Praise for

NEGOTIATION

This book authored by Keld Jensen has the potential to bring about tangible and monetary transformations in your life, without resorting to vague concepts. Unlike other negotiation books that focus solely on optimizing one's own slice of the pie, Jensen's teachings encourage enlarging the entire pie. This approach is wise, as individuals often overlook the opportunity to create more value for all parties involved in their pursuit of personal gain. Don't fall into this trap. Let Jensen's insights guide you toward realizing the full potential of your negotiations.

—Werner Valeur, successful serial entrepreneur

If you're looking for a comprehensive guide to negotiating in a new and revolutionary way, this is the book for you. With practical advice, checklists, and real-life examples, this book provides a step-by-step approach to building strong and sustainable relationships that benefit all parties involved. Highly recommended!

—Mark C. Thompson, World's #1 CEO coach and
New York Times bestselling author

He's done it again! Once more, Keld Jensen provides us with invaluable ideas and approaches to ensure successful negotiations. Practical, easy to read and apply. Essential indeed!

—**Tim Cummins,** President and founder
World Commerce & Contracting

Life is a negotiation, and not very many of us do it well. In this brilliant book you will get all the coaching you need to become a master negotiator. Complete with worksheets and checklists, you too can get to your goals faster and with less conflict. You may not know it, but you need this book! We all do.

—**Chester Elton,** bestselling author of *The Carrot Principle* and
Leading with Gratitude

From a young age, when I started my first job in Schlumberger, I learned the necessity of having the skills of creating a negotiation strategy. When I met Keld Jensen, I learned to put it into a systematic framework, I used it in 20 countries, and with his new book we now learn how to get bigger pizzas through trust, cooperation, and focus. Keld's ability to change the game through his experience and ideas is remarkable and very, very useful when you need to negotiate in a modern world, and you do . . . every day!

—**Jorgen P. Rasmussen,** CEO and President,
Green Therma ApS

Trust is having an existential crisis—yet is an essential ingredient in every successful negotiation. In Keld Jensen's outstanding book, *Negotiation Essentials*, the author cracks the code—and shows the reader how to build trust during intensive negotiations—securing a true win-win for both parties. A must read.

> —**Martin Lindstrom,** *New York Times* bestselling author of
> *Buyology* and *The Ministry of Common Sense*

Negotiation is a psychological game between people; an art and a science that happens both in business and everyday life with family and friends. Jensen discusses the process of negotiation, how negotiation has changed over the years, and introduces the concept of NegoEconomics—the value generated between the gain of one negotiator and the cost of the other.

Smart, concise, and pragmatic, Jensen offers a short, practical guide to the steps you can take to effectively plan for any negotiation or challenging conversation with intelligence, flexibility, and power. Whether you're a senior leader or a stay-at-home parent, this book provides valuable techniques to work with and is packed with sensible, uncomplicated explanations and advice to help with the negotiation process.

> —**Zoe Morton,** CEO, Hundred Brands

Keld Jensen's *Negotiation Essentials* fully delivers on its title, illuminating strategies, tools, and mindsets that are crucial for dealmaking and dispute resolution success.

> —**Michael Wheeler,** Chaired Professor (ret.),
> Harvard Business School

Being a strong supporter of trust-based value creating negotiation philosophy, it's a pleasure to see Keld keeps improving and developing his concepts based on his comprehensive research and experience. There is no such thing as the born negotiator, and this book is relevant for all levels of negotiating. The book provides practical examples, analysis, and useful tools to extract all available value in negotiations. On the shelf with *Getting to Yes*.

—**Jonas Birk Soya Jakobsen**, Vice President—Head of Legal, CESG, and HR, Telenor Procurement Company, Singapore

By embracing the SMARTnership concept and employing the powerful tools shared within the book, you greatly amplify your chances of achieving success, both for yourself and your customer/supplier.

—**Per Holm**, CEO, BlueKolding A/S

For us as a contractor in the construction sector, trust and transparency are the bedrock of our long-term partnerships and the basis for sustainable profitability. And negotiation is the starting point for establishing this trust and transparency, which is why I value Keld Jensen's approach so much. His concepts of NegoEconomics—the added value you can find in negotiations, and SMARTnership—where collaboration is trust-based and transparent, enable you to be more collaborative during negotiations. And in his latest book, Keld explains these concepts in depth, along with sharing helpful insights on topics like cultural sensitivity. His book is a call for companies to be honest, fair, and open during negotiation, and to turn their back on common practices like "not revealing your hand too soon."

—**Aušra Vankevičiūtė**, Group CEO at Staticus

NEGOTIATION
ESSENTIALS

NEGOTIATION ESSENTIALS

THE TOOLS YOU NEED TO FIND COMMON GROUND AND WALK AWAY A WINNER

KELD JENSEN

Mc
Graw
Hill

NEW YORK CHICAGO SAN FRANCISCO ATHENS LONDON

MADRID MEXICO CITY MILAN NEW DELHI

SINGAPORE SYDNEY TORONTO

1 2 3 4 5 6 7 8 9   LCR   28 27 26 25 24 23

ISBN   978-1-265-49543-5
MHID   1-265-49543-2

e-ISBN 978-1-265-49545-9
e-MHID   1-265-49545-9

SMARTnership™ and NegoEconomics™ are trademarks of Keld Jensen.

Library of Congress Cataloging-in-Publication Data

Names: Jensen, Keld, author.
Title: Negotiation essentials : the tools you need to find common ground
  and walk away a winner / Keld Jensen.
Description: New York : McGraw Hill, [2024] | Includes bibliographical
  references and index.
Identifiers: LCCN 2023021136 (print) | LCCN 2023021137 (ebook) | ISBN
  9781265495435 (paperback) | ISBN 9781265495459 (ebook)
Subjects: LCSH: Negotiation in business. | Trust.
Classification: LCC HD58.6 .J396 2024 (print) | LCC HD58.6 (ebook) | DDC
  658.4/052—dc23/eng/20230713
LC record available at https://lccn.loc.gov/2023021136
LC ebook record available at https://lccn.loc.gov/2023021137

McGraw Hill books are available at special quantity discounts to use as premiums and sales promotions or for use in corporate training programs. To contact a representative, please visit the Contact Us pages at www.mhprofessional.com.

McGraw Hill is committed to making our products accessible to all learners. To learn more about the available support and accommodations we offer, please contact us at accessibility@mheducation.com. We also participate in the Access Text Network (www.accesstext.org), and ATN members may submit requests through ATN.

This book is lovingly dedicated to you, the remarkable individual who has not only believed in me but also embraced the transformative power of SMARTnership. As one of the courageous early adopters, you have taken a leap of faith, inspiring me to forge ahead on this journey of innovation and growth. Your unwavering support and trust have propelled me forward, igniting a fire within me to push boundaries and reach new heights. With deep gratitude, I offer this dedication to you, the visionary who has embraced change and played an integral role in shaping the future of SMARTnership.

Contents

PART III

BEYOND THE ESSENTIALS

Acknowledgments

I would like to express my sincere gratitude to the numerous individuals who have contributed to the development of the content presented in this book. Without their support, this project would not have been possible.

To those who have taught me, trained me, and believed in me throughout this journey, I am deeply indebted. As negotiations are best approached as a team effort, it is impossible for me to recognize every person who has played a role in the formation of these ideas.

I want to extend my heartfelt appreciation to those who have entrusted me with the responsibility of sharing knowledge on one of life's most critical skills. I take this responsibility very seriously and have worked diligently to present the best possible information in this book.

I am also grateful for late author and negotiation expert Iwar Unt's influence. He was a critical mentor to me, and the concept upon which my continued work is based was originally designed by him in 1976 in Stockholm, Sweden.

Several individuals deserve special recognition for their contributions to this book. I would like to express my sincere thanks to my content advisor Russ Williams, whose quality control in all my writing is irreplaceable. I would also like to acknowledge the late Paige Stover, my first business agent when I moved to the United States.

Throughout this journey, I have received support and wise counsel from numerous professional colleagues in Europe, Asia, and the

United States. Among them are Tim Cummins from World Commerce & Contracting, Dan Shapiro of the Harvard Program on Negotiation, and the team at McGraw Hill, especially senior editor Cheryl Segura. I am deeply grateful for their recognition of the importance of negotiation. My editor on this book, Dannalie Diaz, has significantly improved the book's readability, and I extend my thanks to her.

A special thank you goes to Per Holm, the CEO of BlueKolding in Denmark, whose company won the Best Tender/Negotiation award of the year based on SMARTnership™ and NegoEconomics™. The award was given by the Organization of Public Procurement Officers. I appreciate how well they have embraced the concept and encourage others to follow their success. Holm is also the father of the three trenches—a model you'll encounter later in this book.

I would like to acknowledge my lifelong friend Antonis for his unwavering support and our cherished friendship.

The content presented in this book was inspired by the presentations, training, meetings, advisory services, and writings of scholars and thought leaders in the fields of negotiation, behavioral economics, and conflict resolution. I have had many friendly debates with my peers, and breakthrough moments have occurred through research and debriefings following difficult negotiation sessions.

One individual, in particular, has been a dear friend and business partner who has been incredibly supportive throughout this journey. I would like to thank Werner Valeur, a successful entrepreneur with numerous exits and a great talent for negotiation.

Lastly, I extend my deepest appreciation to my wife, Keyanna, for her unwavering patience, love, and support. I also want to thank my two sons, Kruise and Kierland, for their love and affection.

This book is dedicated to my late mom—Laura. She meant so much to all of us.

Introduction:
What Is a Negotiation?

Do you negotiate? Of course you do, much more than you may recognize. Many of your daily interactions with others are, in essence, negotiations. I have found that often up to 80 percent of what you believe is communication between two or more individuals, in reality is a negotiation. You talk to a colleague about who should write the report, discuss with your spouse where to go on vacation, or have a dialogue with your kids about whether they should get a dog. At work, you might close a big business deal, sell a customer on a product they were on the fence about, negotiate time off with your boss, or even go back and forth with a potential client on where to meet for a business lunch. But there are other negotiations outside of work that happen every day: deciding what to have for dinner with your spouse, choosing which movie to see at the theater with friends, getting your kids to take out the trash. You negotiate with the dog when he doesn't want to go back in the car after a fun day at the park. Perhaps you even negotiated with yourself about buying this book! Whether you are aware of it or not, I claim that you have 8,000–10,000 negotiations annually.

Some people think that negotiation is something that only takes place in a boardroom and is conducted only by businesspeople in expensive suits. Well, that is one kind of negotiation, surely. But, as you know, anyone involved in any interpersonal relationships, business or otherwise, engages in negotiations all the time. A negotiation could be characterized as a psychological game between people. The factors involved vary from situation to situation, so you should be skilled in the use of a number of negotiating techniques. This enables you to successfully deal with whatever situation arises. The person who masters the art of negotiation is a tremendous asset to a company. The person who is unable to negotiate well may cost a company dearly.

IS NEGOTIATING AN ART OR A SCIENCE?

You've probably heard people talking about "the art of negotiation" or "the science behind negotiating," but what do those phrases truly mean? If negotiation were strictly an art, there could be people born with a talent for it, just as there are natural-born painters, writers, or singers. If negotiation is a science, though, developing its skills would require diligent study and practice.

I believe negotiation is neither strictly science nor art. Rather, it is somewhere in between, with elements of both. Some people take more easily to negotiation than others, yes, but not necessarily because they were born with the talent for negotiating. They are good at it because they enjoy its challenges, demands, and rewards. But even if you are inclined to enjoy negotiating, in order to be effective negotiators we must study and learn, just as we study and learn how to be better writers or solve challenging mathematical equations. And we must recognize that the science and art of negotiation is continually evolving and advancing.

I recently reread the first book I authored, published in 1998, and discovered that some of its content had become outdated. I was surprised to realize that people negotiate differently today than they did 30 years ago. Today's negotiations are faster, less relationship-oriented, more price-focused, and often conclude with less trust and more contract content. It all sounds so unpleasant and impersonal, doesn't it? It's no wonder people feel lost or uneasy with negotiating in their daily lives.

One study I conducted studying 35,000 negotiators globally found that 20 percent of those considered professional negotiators are, in fact, not particularly good at negotiating. One main reason for that is, simply, their dislike of negotiating. So it's wise to ask yourself, "Do I actually enjoy negotiation?" If you do, excellent! Now it's time to make sure you've mastered the skills behind the activity. (And, if you don't much like negotiating, it's just possible that by learning how to negotiate well and practicing it diligently you will discover you're quite good at it after all—and come to enjoy it, too.) That's where this book will help.

WHY READ *THIS* BOOK?

If you google "books on negotiation," the number of results is staggering. People who want to become better negotiators face a deep, dark jungle of books, web content, magazines, blogs, and random advice. Now even artificial intelligence (AI) through ChatGPT offers negotiators free advice. As you make your way through that jungle of information, you're going to find some of it contradictory—which only adds to your challenge. So how do you decide what to read from the endless amount of options? And why should you read this book instead of the countless others out there?

In my 30 years in the industry of negotiation, I've read a great many books on the subject, written by acknowledged authorities in the field. Perhaps you've read a fair number yourself. In all the books I've read, I've run into more than a few by authors who base their advice purely on personal opinion and limited experience. Some books claim to provide solutions to every conceivable negotiating challenge. "Read this book," they say, "and you will be a smashing success. You will win every time!" I don't make quite such an improbable—if not impossible—claim for this book, but I do promise that you'll find plenty here to enhance your understanding of negotiation and advance your ability to succeed as a negotiator. You might even alter your perspective on what constitutes a negotiation.

We'll discuss the difference between negotiating and haggling (and why one is better than the other), how to recognize a negotiation, and how to win it. A unique approach to negotiation in this book is my award-winning concept of NegoEconomics (negotiation economics), or the value generated between the gain of one party and the cost of the other, and the use of SMARTnership strategies, or a partnership where both parties are committed to creating long-term value for each other. We'll be focusing on the importance of Tru$tCurrency, or the capitalization of trust in negotiations, and the 10 important phases in a successful negotiation. I use a lot of examples throughout the book to showcase the concepts I talk about. You'll notice most of those examples are between a buyer and a seller. You might be thinking, *Well, that doesn't apply to me because I'm not a buyer or seller at work*. But I believe we are all buyers and sellers. When you are trying to convince your spouse where to go on vacation or your kids to do their chores, you must convince them to buy what you're selling.

A DIFFERENT WAY TO THINK
ABOUT NEGOTIATION

As a negotiator, have you felt the need to be armed to the teeth with tools and techniques to outmaneuver and triumph over your counterpart? Have you thought of negotiation as a game to be won at any cost, at the other side's expense? Have you regarded negotiation more as a life-and-death hostage situation where you face a desperate opponent? Some negotiators approach negotiations as outright conflicts, or they fear some sort of conflict is almost certain to arise. They assume in advance that their negotiating counterpart is eager for a contest or competition, or to engage in conflict for its own sake. A procurement officer evaluating a supplier might assume the supplier will be insistent that they are the best option, so the officer might enter the negotiation ready to fight off pressure. And so, these negotiators are continually wary and always on their guard. They are on the defensive from the start, sometimes even argumentative, without any real-world evidence to justify it.

It's my view that we should all work in the direction of sincere collaboration and more frictionless and fruitful negotiations. Yes, there will inevitably be disagreements and differences of opinion. But these need not and should not be viewed as threats. Approached calmly and intelligently, they can reveal unforeseen opportunities and pathways to progress. This is employing negotiation as a tool to discover and harvest the potential *benefits* of disagreements and differences of opinion, rather than using it to subdue the other party.

We all depend on others in our efforts to reach our goals, solve our problems, and satisfy our needs. The real-world situations we face are rarely black-and-white. Others sometimes doubt or argue about things we believe to be right. Effective negotiation will lead us to sound decisions when dealing with the following examples:

- Your boss offers a lower pay raise than expected.

- You need to increase your prices on services you provide.

- Your supplier's product delivery time wasn't what was agreed to.

- The airline will not refund your ticket for missing a flight due to a connection delay.

- You are negotiating a new job or promotion.

- You have your annual contract negotiation with an existing client.

- Your phone rings and your client is threatening to go to a cheaper supplier if you don't lower your prices.

- You want to go to Greece for vacation and your spouse wants to go to California.

More and more professional negotiators have discovered that *cooperation* produces superior results and promotes more durable relationships. Many organizations understand that developing an effective negotiating strategy is every bit as vital as having proven sales, communication, or even marketing strategies. A great negotiation strategy truly is a management necessity.

BRING A LARGER PIZZA TO THE TABLE

A vital element in any negotiating strategy—and for any individual negotiator seeking to be maximally effective in their negotiations—is to put your intelligence and energy to work to create added value. I call this NegoEconomics, which we'll discuss further in later chapters. Imagine you're ordering a pizza for your hungry family of five. You order a medium pizza that comes with eight slices. But everyone is really hungry—one slice each isn't going to cut it, and you'll end up fighting over the extra slices. Instead you could order a large and guarantee two slices for each of you. Or you could come to the table with a large and a medium, and potentially have leftovers! The idea is to make the "pizza" larger so there's more to be shared. If you have a sufficiently ample pizza, you emerge with the best sort of victory, one with *two* big winners—you and your family.

Negotiators who meet in open dialogue stand to discover unforeseen opportunities for increased profits and minimized risks. They do so by seeking out and exploiting the unseen, unutilized differences between the two parties—the asymmetric value. For example, two companies are negotiating a contract, and one company's cost of capital is 3 percent and the other company's cost of capital is 7 percent. The difference between the two companies' cost of capital is 4 percent, which in this case is the NegoEconomics. To capitalize that difference the company with the 3 percent cost of capital would finance the deal and get compensated by the counterpart. That in turn grows the "pizza" and results in greater abundance to be shared by both sides. Discovering, realizing, and sharing that abundance is what NegoEconomics is all about.

RECOGNIZING THE VALUE OF TEAMWORK IS KEY TO NEGOTIATION

We must realize that we are still negotiating in the same way we did in 1776. Sure, we do have a bunch of technology to support our negotiations today. We can negotiate online and through email and conference/video calls. Yet, we haven't really *matured* the techniques we use for negotiation. We're still bogged down in zero-sum games where one party wins at the expense of the other.

Why is this? In so many books, the advice negotiation trainers and advisors offer will only make the horse and the buggy go faster. Instead, we should switch to a car, perhaps even an electric vehicle. Instead of just adding clever techniques and smart psychological tools to outsmart the counterpart in a negotiation, essentially making it a fight where only one party leaves victorious, we should change our way of thinking and look at negotiation as a team effort. Teamwork in this context means that negotiators strive to make each other successful without either one sacrificing their own success. Is that really possible? Yes, but not always easy—and it requires an educated negotiator who really understands the concept of collaboration.

> If two people always agree, it's a sign that at least one of them isn't thinking critically or being completely honest.

I must caution you that my approach to

negotiation differs somewhat from the norm. My approach recommends openness, honesty, transparency, and collaboration. Reading this book may provoke and challenge you, but my primary aim is to change and enhance your understanding of what negotiation truly entails. It's not just about creating winners on one or both sides of the table but using NegoEconomics to benefit both parties in any negotiation. While some will criticize this approach as being naive, it remains one of the most awarded negotiation strategies worldwide and has consistently yielded successful results, not just around the table, but around the world.

Regardless of your current beliefs about what negotiation is or should be, I invite you to explore and experience the negotiating philosophy, approaches, and methods I've found, through long and voluminous experience, to be the most effective. I've gathered them together for you in this book, along with a practical toolbox of techniques, all to make you a more effective, successful negotiator.

HOW THIS BOOK IS ORGANIZED

This book is conveniently divided into three parts that will guide you through your negotiations in a practical, accessible way.

In Part I, "The Essentials," you'll explore what makes a great negotiator, the importance of trust, what to do if you think you're losing a negotiation, and negotiating virtually and internationally.

Moving into Part II, "The Essentials Applied," you'll complete a preliminary benchmark assessment to help you target opportunities for growth. Then you'll be directed through the prenegotiation phases, the phases in the negotiation, and the postnegotiation phase, plus the five different negotiation styles.

In Part III, "Beyond the Essentials," you'll find valuable information about the award-winning negotiation model called NegoEconomics, explaining how you can increase the value in every negotiation.

I hope you'll find this book to be comprehensive and compelling. Are you ready to get started?

Remember, the objective in any negotiation should be a total realized value greater than the sum of its parts. You can achieve that, and you can achieve it consistently. The world will be better for it.

Welcome to *Negotiation Essentials*.

PART I

THE ESSENTIALS

What Makes a Great Negotiator?

Teddy Roosevelt was about to start his presidential campaign tour. Shortly before embarking on a long train trip, his campaign management discovered a serious problem. They had already printed three million copies of a campaign pamphlet with Roosevelt's picture and boxed and carefully loaded them onto the train, only to realize that they had not secured permission from Moffett Studios, holder of the copyright on the picture. Quick research showed if they distributed the pamphlets, they could be liable for $1 in damages per picture— a potential $3 million loss. It seemed like a lose-lose situation. If they destroyed the pamphlets, they would risk losing the election, but if they paid the $3 million, the campaign would be bankrupt. How would you negotiate this, knowing Moffett Studios was hard-pressed for money and wouldn't be lenient?

Campaign manager George Perkins contacted Moffett with this cable:

> We are planning to distribute millions of pamphlets with
> Roosevelt's picture on the cover. It will be great publicity
> for the studio whose photograph we use. How much will
> you pay us to use yours? Respond immediately.

Moffett Studios replied that although they'd never done something like that before, they would be willing to pay $250. If Perkins had appealed to Moffett Studios for leniency, the campaign would've ended up paying a fortune to the studio and losing the election. Moffett Studios likely wouldn't have been lenient. It's not every day that a grave error that leads to your own fortune falls in your lap! But Perkins was smart enough to recognize one key thing: Moffett Studios didn't know what the campaign's next best alternative (NBA) was.

In this case, the campaign's NBA to discovering the copyright issue was to pay up and lose. Moffett Studios' NBA, if the campaign refused to pay, was to send them to court and win. Perkins was able to recognize that and think outside the box.

Too often, negotiators forget the other party may not see the full picture and may not know your NBA. If you know theirs, you may be able to control the negotiation and win.

THE MARKINGS OF A GREAT NEGOTIATOR

Just having negotiation experience doesn't guarantee that someone is a skilled negotiator. Some people believe that having a certain number of years of experience automatically makes them an expert, but that's not necessarily the case. I've come across negotiators who claim to have extensive experience but who just repeat the same negotiation formula in every deal. As we'll learn, one key to a great negotiation is to listen and find all potential values in each negotiation. This means every negotiation is different—what works for one may not work for another. A good negotiator is aware that asymmetric value can be found in a negotiation. A great negotiator asks questions instead of arguing, focuses on their counterpart's value and costs, and is transparent and shares values with that counterpart without conceding too much.

During my research, I observed a variety of negotiations and noticed recurring patterns among the most successful negotiators. Next, let's look at the patterns I've found to make a great negotiator.

Be confident

They Have Analyzed the Negotiation Variables

While preparing for negotiations, great negotiators work out a list of all possible variables that may be discussed. After analyzing the variables, they determine what variables are nonnegotiable for them, where they can compromise, and what outcomes occur if they compromise. They also don't limit their focus to one variable.

For example, two suppliers offer the same product; supplier A offers it at $40/unit and supplier B at $41/unit. Since $40 is less than $41, it's the better deal, right? But supplier A also requires advance payment while supplier B does not. The purchasing company would spend more on interest by financing the full amount supplier A requires up front, making it a worse deal than if the company had gone with supplier B. By limiting their focus to price rather than considering other variables like full payment and interest rate, the company risks losing more.

To become a great negotiator, you must have a good grasp of a deal's economics—how will this negotiation affect the budget? But a great negotiator doesn't forget about the soft variables—those that cannot be measured with the usual economic or technical goals. A tenant trying to save money may negotiate a lower rent price for a fourth-floor apartment of a walkup rather than the first floor, the soft variable being where the apartment is located in this example. Other soft variables include the people in the negotiation (customers, partners, negotiating counterparts), interpersonal relationships with the other party (and how those can be affected by the negotiation), timelines, and emotions like insecurity or anxiety over losing a deal.

Great negotiators also prioritize variables and recognize when conceding a point helps them win another. Let's say you are negotiating a reduction in delivery time with a customer. Instead of just focusing on that one variable (figuring out how many days to reduce delivery time by), you could offer a reduction in delivery time *if* you're able to increase price by 1 percent. By adding that extra factor, you're able to look at the overall picture in any negotiation to ensure you walk away from the table with the best deal you can get.

One mistake less successful negotiators make is to look at a negotiation as one-sided, where they have to win at all costs. In doing so, they risk losing more. For example, an employee asks the boss about adjusting her in-office schedule. Currently, the employee comes in five days a week but wants to work from home permanently. The boss is adamant that company policy is to be in the office at least some days a week. However, the employee really enjoys the freedom of being at home. She argues she gets the same amount of work done regardless of her location and it's not fair to have to commute in when other companies allow remote work. The boss responds that maybe she should find a job in one of those other companies, effectively shutting down the conversation.

What went wrong? The employee wasn't able to see the value of flexibility and ended up losing her bid to work from home (and walking away with a veiled threat on her job!). She thought only about her half of the negotiation, and didn't listen when her boss said it was a company requirement to be in the office *at least some days a week*. How could this employee have been a better negotiator? She could have suggested a hybrid schedule, perhaps only coming in three days a week. Yes, she's conceding on her goal to work remote all five days, but she could pick which days to commute in. If she works from home Monday and Friday, she doesn't have to get out of bed early after a great weekend to make her commute. Instead she can roll out in her pajamas five minutes before start time and log on. Or, she can recognize that many people choose Mondays/Fridays as their work-from-home days, so she can instead choose Tuesdays and Thursdays and enjoy an easier commute on Mondays and Fridays. By considering more options, she can find other values to help her toward her ultimate goal of *not commuting every day*.

Knowing when to stand firm while recognizing where to be flexible and compromise are the marks of a great negotiator.

They Write Out Details Before a Negotiation, and Use Visual Aids During

When preparing for a negotiation (see Chapter 6), a great negotiator creates an overview of the details of an upcoming negotiation. Write down what the variables are, what your ultimate goal is, and the steps you plan to get there. Visualizing your goal helps prevent you from straying from it. It also helps you find where you can compromise and collaborate to reach a desired goal. Writing out your plan helps you see where there is room for bargaining as well as which parts of the negotiation are connected. In an inverse of the previous example, a customer can connect a demand for shorter delivery times to a payment demand from the store owner by recognizing that offering a bigger advance payment might get the desired delivery time. This, of course, only works if you're biggest goal is delivery time, not cost saving. As discussed later in the book, never concede so much that you lose more than you offer.

Successful negotiators also use visual aids during a negotiation to present their points. Effective visual aids clearly communicate goals and desired outcomes to the other party. Use a flip chart, whiteboard, electronic board, shared PowerPoint, or even paper to lay out the points you've already worked on when outlining the negotiation in the preparation stage.

They Show Initiative During Negotiations

A great negotiator isn't the one who speaks or argues the most. Great negotiators show initiative by listening to the other party, asking questions, and following up on points mentioned. This allows them to have a clearer picture of how they can achieve their ultimate goal. A negotiator skilled at procuring information can find out which variables are negotiable and what the outcome looks like if those variables are negotiated. A skilled negotiator who suspects a customer would benefit from a shorter delivery time won't simply ask, "How much could you make if we shortened the delivery time by one month?" Instead that negotiator opens a discussion about costs incurred from shortening the delivery time, what would be gained in return for granting the shorter delivery date, what the consequences of missing the shorter delivery date would be, and so on.

Many negotiators believe if they don't reveal too much, they can avoid giving the opponent the upper hand. But this only works if you aren't clear on the details of a negotiation, or if the opponent takes the bait and gives a lot more in their eagerness to close the deal. That strategy also runs the risk of creating distrust between parties. Or it could generate boredom if the other party perceives this as an attempt to slow down negotiations. Your counterpart could ultimately walk away before you even truly begin negotiating.

A great negotiator recognizes that negotiating is about give and take. If you want something, be prepared to give something in return. If you want information, what kind of information can you give? A great negotiator has the courage to take the first step and open up. However, be wary of putting all your cards on the table without getting anything in return.

Though great negotiators don't argue a lot, they still stand up for their demands. They often take the initiative to make the first offer. If the other negotiating party says no to any demand, great negotiators don't simply accept it and move on to the next point. They spend more time asking questions, mapping out scenarios, and making counteroffers to achieve a beneficial result.

They Are Good at Communicating

Communication is key in any negotiation, as it is in any aspect of business. A great negotiator communicates points clearly, confidently, and in detail. The best negotiators are good listeners and ask questions, listening not only to the words spoken but also for the unspoken value. Imagine your counterpart saying, "We want an earlier delivery." The great negotiator doesn't jump into a concession to give an earlier delivery away for free nor start arguing why an earlier delivery isn't possible. Instead that person picks up on the subtle signal that the variable of delivery time carries a value for the counterpart and responds by asking, "What do you gain if we do change delivery time?"

Good negotiators also excel at giving presentations and illustrating their demands, the advantages available to the other party, and what alternatives are available. Being a great negotiator and communicator requires that you like being in the spotlight. If being in the spotlight isn't your thing, consider negotiating as part of a team and taking on the role of someone who assists the person in the spotlight.

They Have High, but Realistic, Goals

Great negotiators have ambitious goals and strive to do better than their NBA. But they're also realistic. They know how to find the middle ground between an insultingly low offer and an astronomically high offer. And, importantly, they can back up their ambitious demands with credible, well-researched arguments. What also makes them realistic is the ability to adjust their goals based on how the negotiation goes. Let's say you are buying a new Apple Mac computer. An unrealistic goal is to expect a 20 percent discount. You haven't done your preparation properly if you neglected to research how much Macs are selling for and what discounts are being offered. A more realistic goal could be to ask for a free pair of Apple Air Pods if purchasing a MacBook. At times, great negotiators put off specifying their goals until they know their counterparts' strengths and goals better.

Negotiators who aim too low, who only strive to reach an offer only slightly better than what they're being offered, or who are afraid of taking a risk because they want to stay within budget or not risk losing too much, ultimately leave a lot of money on the negotiating table.

Consider a customer who wants to buy a new car and has a maximum budget of $30,500 but would prefer to go lower. At the dealership, he tests a few cars, asks the salesperson lots of questions, and ultimately falls in love with a sedan that meets his needs. The price is $31,000, and he says this is above his budget. The salesperson asks him to wait while she checks with her manager. After a moment, she comes back to match his $30,500 budget. Satisfied, the customer drives away with his new car. But when he looks over while at a stoplight, he spots a competitor who has his car with the sticker price he just paid: $30,500! If the customer had shopped around more, he might have gotten the competitor's car for $30,000. Or he could've gone back to the original dealership with the competitor's $30,000 price and gotten an even better price! The customer failed to aim high enough and, as a result, is now feeling swindled and unsatisfied.

They Cut to the Chase

Instead of wasting time arguing, great negotiators lay out their points in detail, supporting their offers or demands and explaining how the other party benefits from their conditions. They also don't jump into counterarguments without first fully understanding the opponent's priorities. A negotiator should be open to giving and receiving information and understand that sometimes concessions are necessary to reach a desired outcome.

Instead of getting bogged down by small details, the best negotiators focus on the important points. They know if opponents can agree on important details, all other things will come into place. Sometimes giving in on small details is beneficial to gaining a larger piece of the pie. But the best recognize that giving in is not one-sided. All concessions they make are small enough that it won't hurt their overall goal, and they make sure they get something in return for any concession.

They Suggest Alternate Solutions and Create a Positive Climate

When great negotiators run into pushback on any particular point, they suggest alternative solutions instead of getting defensive, pushy, or completely shutting down. They understand that coming to a conclusion calmly and rationally rather than by force leads to a much better outcome. Consider one of *Aesop's Fables*, "The North Wind and the Sun." A traveler wrapped in a cloak is passing by, and the Sun challenges the North Wind to remove the traveler's cloak and prove which of the two of them is stronger. When the Wind tries to blow the cloak off the traveler, he only holds on tighter. But when the Sun warms him, he willingly takes it off. In the same way, a negotiator who approaches the negotiation with warmth is more successful than one who tries to use force, threats, or power games. A negotiator who uses warmth would say, "That was an interesting proposal, but how do you propose to arrange financing?" rather than "That was an insulting proposal, and I will walk away right now if you don't pay me what I want."

Great negotiators understand the importance of mutual respect and treat the other party with respect and understanding, as an equal partner in the negotiation. They don't pressure, cajole, or insult. Treating the other party like an inferior only causes that person to push back, or worse, walk away entirely. Whom are you more likely to continue to do business with: an insurance company representative who insinuates you are to blame for your accident or one who is compassionate and asks questions to understand how to best help you?

The best negotiators also understand that while it's important to build trust and respect, they don't put their own demands second. Being understanding doesn't mean being weak. On the contrary, you show emotional and professional strength when expressing your demands calmly, rationally, and respectfully. They also acknowledge the importance of building credibility. Being truthful, open, and avoiding psychological pressure or games all build to a better negotiation experience for all parties involved. We'll learn more about building trust and mutual respect in Chapter 2.

They Have a Strategy and Work Methodically

Entering any negotiation with a strategy is key. Showing up with a strategy shows initiative, builds your confidence, and helps you guide the conversation in the way you want. Looking at strategy options, you can pick between positional (zero-sum), where only one negotiating party wins, or collaboration (partnership/SMARTnership—SMARTnership is partnership version 2.0 adding rules of the game, variables, Nego-Economics, and trust), where both parties work together to achieve a successful result. Instead of having a strategy, many improvise. They run the risk of missing the chance to make new offers or counteroffers. With structure and strategy, you can determine whether you should make one overall offer covering all parts of the agreement, or whether you should handle problems one at a time. Not knowing this ahead of time can cause you to become stressed and flustered, which is when most mistakes are made!

A negotiator who has a strategy knows the advantages and disadvantages of making a first offer, or how to not make one-sided concessions. But while having a strategy is important, remain flexible. Your approach may have to change depending on how the negotiation is going. If your counterpart is asking for a longer warranty period than you expected, you'll need to have a plan B ready. If you are unable to offer a longer warranty period, prepare what you can offer instead: faster delivery, better service, education, different payment terms, and so on.

Great negotiators are also structured and methodical. Always enter a negotiation with an agenda (see Chapter 6), and take copious notes for reference. Do not jump back and forth between individual points but rather negotiate every single point until there is nothing more to discuss. Before going to the next point, sum up to make sure all parties understand each other correctly.

Great negotiators don't waste time. If the strategy they are using isn't working, they aren't afraid to switch it up and see what works.

They Assign Roles If Working in a Team

If you're negotiating as part of a team, it's important to be clear on the division of roles. You should at least have these roles in the group:

> **Negotiation leader:** Choose the person who is the best communicator, not necessarily the boss or manager. This person speaks for the group.

Listener/observer: Choose someone with sufficient experience to understand the terms and what the company is looking to win from the negotiation. This person should, if possible, sit somewhat away from the negotiation table and take continuous notes. During each break the observer provides the others with a picture of how the negotiations are progressing, what signals the opponent is sending out, and how the opponent has reacted to the negotiation leader's own propositions. The negotiation leader must be able to use the observer for summaries during the negotiations.

Calculator: This person manages "the economy" by making calculations and keeping track of how any change of conditions being discussed affects the overall result. What are we giving away? What are we receiving? What do the opponent's demands entail? How large a scope is left? Where are we now in the negotiations in relation to our goals?

Great negotiators know to stick to their roles. If they are not the team leader, they will not jump in to lead the conversation. Instead, they are supportive by calling for a break to regroup if the team leader gets stuck on a point.

Agreeing on how the group will communicate during the negotiation is also important when working in a team. Some of the most common communication tools used are hand or face signals (such as a thumbs-up, subtle nod, or wink), eye contact, small written notes, and breaks.

They Take a Beat to Evaluate

Great negotiators don't cave to time pressure. "You'll have to make a decision now or I'm walking away from the offer" doesn't faze them. Even if the offer is good and within the goal set up, a great negotiator takes one last break to check the terms: "This offer has great potential and I think it would benefit both of us. I want to make sure we'll both be happy with the outcome; could I take a day or two to review the terms?"

If working in a team, check with team members to make sure everyone approves the agreement and review any meeting notes.

PRACTICE MAKES PERFECT

Many who fail at negotiating do so because they are underprepared or don't know how to analyze the situation during a negotiation. To be a great negotiator, one has to put a lot of energy on mapping out all possibilities presented, learn to bargain instead of argue, and continuously improve communication skills. You don't automatically become better at negotiating simply by getting a theoretical knowledge of negotiation. That is only the beginning! Fine-tune your negotiation skills through practical negotiation exercises (a simple google search will give you many options) as well as real negotiations.

ESSENTIAL TAKEAWAYS

At the end of each chapter, you'll find Essential Takeaways. These are the most important points you'll need to carry into your professional life to find lasting success. In this chapter, the Essential Takeaways are:

- A great negotiator is one who:
    - Listens to their counterpart
    - Asks questions
    - Is aware of all variables in the negotiation
    - Prepares ahead of time
    - Comes into a negotiation with a strategy
- If negotiating in a team, have a negotiating leader, a listener/observer, and someone who manages "the economy."
- Becoming a great negotiator takes practice. .

The Importance of Trust in Negotiation

In a simple experiment involving more than 3,000 individuals worldwide, I examined the significance of trust.

Participants were presented with a straightforward decision: purchase plastic water bottles for their operations from their existing supplier, supplier A, whom they like, trust, and have had a great relationship with over the past five years, or choose a new supplier, supplier B, whom they do not trust or like, but who is offering the exact same product at a 2 percent lower price.

The vast majority of respondents, 97 percent, chose to continue buying from supplier A, despite the minor price difference.

To further explore this phenomenon, I increased the price difference by 1 percent each time and asked participants which supplier they would prefer to do business with. My findings indicated that most people have a pain threshold (or how far they can go before conceding on a point) of 10 to 20 percent before they would consider choosing supplier B, even though they do not trust or like that supplier. Some individuals even went as high as 30 percent before choosing the new supplier. Additionally, the greater the complexity of a product or service, the more important trust and likeability became.[1]

Trust is absolutely essential in any important long-term relationship and negotiation, whether you are selling, buying, resolving conflict, or negotiating solutions. It is difficult to establish an effective business framework if there is no trust between the parties seeking to work together. Very few people want to do business with people or companies they cannot trust, even if they offer the lowest prices. Likewise, very few people want to work with a colleague they cannot rely on.

TRUST AS MONETARY VALUE

Consulting firm A. T. Kearney carried out a study that confirmed the central role of trust in negotiations.[2] A direct link exists between trust and profit. The more trust you're able to bring to the table, the more money you are likely to walk away with. This means, provided you continually share information with your negotiation counterpart in an honest and open manner, not only will trust increase considerably, but so will the quality of the agreement and the potential for optimizing financial prospects. The ability to build solid, trustworthy relationships is increasingly seen as a vital competitive advantage.

Economists have calculated that physical capital (e.g., infrastructure) accounts for one-fourth of our wealth. My experience shows that human capital (e.g., education level, ideas, and innovative actions) account for roughly another 50 percent. Until recently, no one has convincingly accounted for the remaining 25 percent.

I believe the other 25 percent can be found where economists rarely look: trust. The Scandinavian society is remarkable for its high trust level, and that abundant trust is arguably the basis of the region's enviable wealth and happiness. (Denmark, for example, has ranked high in the World Happiness Report as one of the world's happiest nations several years in a row.[3]) The smaller you view the risk of being conned by a stranger, the easier it is to cooperate with a stranger—or an organization about which you do not have complete information.

Numerous studies carried out in Europe and the United States indicate lack of trust is a direct cause of unprofitable agreements and the loss of business opportunities. There are plenty of examples of the difficulties created when trust and respect are absent from a negotiating environment. Good relationships lay the groundwork for a profitable future. The more an agreement is based on trust, the greater the likelihood it will be implemented. Without trust and understanding, the parties have no more than an empty agreement that may or may not translate into a productive business relationship.

My brother Leif shared a story about his experience remodeling his newly purchased home. During the remodeling process, my brother purchased a new kitchen from a large manufacturer and a wood stove from a small, family-owned local business. The two suppliers differed vastly in size and approach. The large kitchen supplier demanded full payment up front despite the components not being in stock and the delivery time exceeding 10 weeks. They also required my brother to be present for a four-hour delivery window, making the process arduous and complicated.

Conversely, the family-owned wood stove supplier didn't require any up-front payment, had the stove in stock, and was flexible with delivery and installation. My brother texted his preferred date, and the supplier responded by asking for access to the house and installation instructions. On the agreed delivery date, my brother and his wife left for work and later received a text message from the supplier stating, "Wood stove installed." My brother wasn't even required to be present during the delivery and installation process. When my brother returned home, he found the stove had been installed perfectly, and the supplier had left a handwritten invoice requesting payment within a few days. Meanwhile, the kitchen supplier delivered the wrong parts despite their superior warehouse and logistical systems, resulting in additional costs and delays.

This story sheds light on the impact of trust and efficiency in negotiations, customer satisfaction, and overall experience. It highlights the concept of transactional costs: when trust is high, transactional costs are low and profits increase. On the other hand, when trust is low, transactional costs increase and profits decrease. The wood stove supplier had low transactional costs, and the process was smooth and frictionless due to the high level of trust between the parties. The kitchen supplier, on the other hand, had high transactional costs, including paperwork, up-front payments, lengthy delivery times, and delivery windows, all of which led to additional complications and expenses.

It's essential to prioritize trust and efficiency when evaluating business practices to enhance customer experience and contribute to the overall success of your business. This story took place in Denmark, a country known for its exceptional societal trust. In this country, my brother had no qualms about leaving the key for an unfamiliar supplier, and the supplier, in turn, had no concerns about delivering and installing without receiving payment up front. The transactional cost was minimal, and the saved time proved to be valuable for all parties involved.

Consider how you can replicate similar scenarios to prioritize trust and efficiency and benefit your business.

PREREQUISITES FOR A SMARTnership

There are a number of basic prerequisites to the formation of a cooperative negotiation climate, but the two main ones are interpersonal chemistry and generosity. The presence of these elements will ensure the proper environment for a collaborative negotiation is developed. These factors enhance the probability Tru$tCurrency will be successfully infused into a negotiation.

Interpersonal Chemistry

If there is no interpersonal chemistry between the parties in a negotiation, the trust factor will not emerge. Interpersonal chemistry is demonstrated through humility, mutual respect, trust, and openness.

Though critical, these attributes are not always sufficient. Enthusiasm and a positive attitude also play a major role in creating trust. Deals are made between people. People require an interpersonal dynamic that facilitates openness and a free flow of information. If the signals customarily sent by people who want to establish good rapport—such as eye contact and inclusive gestures—are absent, it is almost impossible to build a foundation for the infusion of the trust factor.

A negotiation dynamic is built on trust, cooperation, open and honest communication between the parties, and a willingness to listen to and understand each other's needs and requirements. When the negotiator's actions are inconsistent with his or her words, the other party loses trust and becomes reluctant to continue the bargaining process. A reluctance to engage socially and emotionally can also create failures in communication. When opposite these personality types, delegates will have to work particularly hard to facilitate constructive dialogue and to build a foundation for cooperation and trust.

Lack of sympathy, understanding, and respect for cultural differences can also limit the space for success in negotiations. For instance, Eastern negotiators may assume Western negotiators will be combative and operate primarily using a zero-sum strategy. It is important Western negotiators dispel this preconception in order to generate a cooperative environment. (More on negotiating abroad in Chapter 5.)

Daniel Kahneman, Princeton professor and renowned psychologist, author, and researcher in the field of behavioral economics, is widely recognized as one of the foremost experts in this area. Despite not being an economist himself, he was awarded the Nobel Prize in economics in recognition of his groundbreaking research. Kahneman's work has been particularly notable for his conclusion that human beings are inherently irrational, and that the concept of a completely rational person is, in fact, a fallacy. This insight, which formed the basis of his Nobel Prize–winning research, has had a profound impact on the field of economics and beyond.

The orthodox economist may not agree with the idea that we prefer doing business with someone we like and trust, even if their product is inferior and more expensive than a competitor's superior product. This is because concepts such as sympathy, trust, and confidence are not typically included in rational economic models that rely on spreadsheets and quantitative analysis.

However, according to Kahneman's research, all our decisions, whether it's buying a new car, choosing a job, selecting a supplier, or finding a spouse, are fundamentally based on emotions.[4] We first make an emotional decision and then seek out facts to support our choice.

This means that emotions play a crucial role in our decision-making process, and we often document our choices with supporting facts later.

When I share the fact that human beings are inherently irrational with managers in my work, I often encounter resistance. Many people don't like to think of themselves as irrational, and there seems to be a taboo around admitting to it. However, if we accept Kahneman's conclusion that we are all irrational, it opens up a whole new way of thinking about business. Suddenly, product, price, quality, and delivery time become secondary considerations. What's really important is *people*. Relationships and trust become more important than the specifics of the deal. All business is ultimately about people, and the most successful negotiators understand this fundamental truth.

Generosity

In negotiations, givers are smarter than takers.

Many people find it difficult to be generous. Their own assessment of what constitutes fair compensation, or a fair price, is, more often than not, nonnegotiable. They become indignant and take on a "who do you think you are" attitude. If you try to eliminate your opponent's ability to turn a profit, you're cutting off your nose to spite your face. Your counterpart will come to resent you and the organization you represent. And it's possible when it comes to future transactions, that person will look for another partner.

In a *New York Times* article, Adam Grant, an organizational psychologist at the Wharton School of the University of Pennsylvania, argues that generous people are more intelligent than people who are only in it for themselves.[5] For example, one of my personal friends and business clients, Thomas, is a tough, hard-nosed negotiator. A few years ago, he was purchasing a company being sold by a Swede. The negotiations took place over a period of months through meetings, emails, and telephone calls. As the months went on, Thomas noticed that his counterpart was losing focus. He was making mental mistakes regarding the details of the deal and began unconditionally accepting Thomas's proposals.

While many negotiators would have taken advantage of the situation, Thomas decided to confront his counterpart about his behavior. To his amazement, the Swede opened up that his wife had been diagnosed with cancer and was receiving treatment. Thomas could have closed the deal by taking advantage of his counterpart's distraction, but instead he chose to delay the negotiations. In the end he signed the agreement for a fair price so that his counterpart still made a profit. Thomas was able to complete the deal, but he got much more than that. He earned a lifelong friend and an advocate who would sing his praises to anyone around him.

In today's world of internet business relationships, fast-paced dealmaking, low trust, and a single-minded focus on price, there is nothing more powerful than a display of generosity. It creates such a strong human emotion. People will quickly trust you and be more willing to cooperate when they see you are operating with good intentions. They spread the word, offer you referrals, and bring repeated business. It creates an environment for more open, honest, and transparent negotiations to take place. And the creativity that results leads to more valuable outcomes.

South African anti-apartheid activist and politician Nelson Mandela once said, "A good head and a good heart are always a formidable combination." My call to action for you: maintain your generosity throughout everything you do and seek to incorporate it into your career and daily life. Generosity is not a sign of weakness. It can be one of your greatest strengths if you have the courage to show it. And by sharing your generosity with others, you allow the rest of the world to do the same.

INSIST ON YOUR COUNTERPART WINNING TOO

The incompetent purchaser says, "If the supplier has made a profit from the deal, we have *not* done our job." The relationship between buyer and seller should be one of mutual benefit. Neither can succeed without the efforts of the other. Smart purchasing professionals recognize this and allow their suppliers to earn money. Really smart purchasers go one step further and demand that the supplier make a healthy profit on the transaction.

NegoEconomics requires that you demonstrate generosity when it is time to share the gains that have emerged in the course of the negotiation. Such behavior will enable you to earn Tru$tCurrency and ensure the likelihood of future business with your counterpart. Keeping your allies alive and financially successful is just as vital as succeeding yourself. However, such generosity can be difficult to practice.

ESSENTIAL TAKEAWAYS

- Generate trust and interpersonal connection in your negotiations.
- Trust can be quantified into monetary value.
- Verbalize trust in the code of conduct you use for your negotiations.

How to Tell if You're Losing a Negotiation—and Win It Back

A negotiation can be made or broken depending on which few basic strategies and tools you use, and which ones the other party uses. You may enter a negotiation confident in your talking points, but halfway through may find yourself conceding more than you planned. Too often, negotiators don't pick up on the hints they're about to lose a negotiation until it is too late. You definitely want to be the one in the driver's seat—not the one holding on for dear life in the passenger side. There are six key signs you're lagging behind and headed for a lost negotiation.

The other side is in the driver's seat if they are...

Setting the agenda

Controlling the flow of the negotiation

Asking questions rather than making statements

Keeping their cards hidden

Breezing through the process without breaking a sweat

Presenting the initial offer

SETTING THE AGENDA

It's a common misconception that the party hosting a meeting is entitled to set and control the agenda. The visiting party is supposed to go along with whatever steps the host announces. I strongly advise you not to agree to or allow it. Blindly accepting the other side's agenda is handing them control of the proceedings, and letting them set the rules. The agenda is often—and should be—the subject of your first encounter with a counterpart, even before the main negotiation begins.

If, at any point in the negotiation, your counterpart has taken control of the agenda, it means you are losing your grip on the process. Many a negotiator has failed based on just this one factor. What tells you that your counterpart has seized control of the agenda? Here are some examples:

- Your counterpart opens the meeting by presenting your team with a printed agenda, saying they put it together to save you the time and trouble.

- An agreed-upon agenda was set before negotiations began, but your counterpart arrives with a flipchart or PowerPoint detailing the agenda items and sequence, and puts a member of his or her team in charge of it to monitor and control the proceedings.

- As a negotiation progresses, your counterpart doesn't respect the order laid out in the agenda. Instead, the person jumps around in the agreed-upon sequence to better suit his or her interests.

So, how can you prevent this?

- Never blindly accept a counterpart's agenda. Insist on negotiating the content and order of the proceedings before any other step.

- Prepare your own proposed agenda in advance, and be ready to present and negotiate it at the outset of the proceedings.

- Take the initiative to manage the flipchart or PowerPoint that visualizes the set agenda.

CONTROLLING THE FLOW OF THE NEGOTIATION

Do you typically take the initiative in a negotiation, or does your counterpart most often take it? Do you open the negotiation by introducing the agenda or variables to be discussed, or is it more often the other party?

This is a bit of a generalization, but in most cases you should take the initiative. If your counterpart is repeatedly calling the shots (e.g., what variable is to be negotiated next), call for a break. Have a discussion with your team about how to break up the counterpart-dominated flow.

You see this often in sports. During a basketball game, a coach may call a time-out not only to replace players, but also to strategize. Sometimes it's a means of disrupting the other team's flow, slowing them down when they're ahead and the momentum is going their way.

Controlling the flow doesn't have to mean being aggressive or even combative. You can be in control yet still be quite open and transparent, asking plenty of questions. A potential customer might say, "We want to discuss your hourly rate!" Your reply as a skilled negotiator could be "Why? Is there some added value or cost for you, if the terms changed?" An aggressive counterpart might reply, "That's none of your business. We just want to know what you are capable of!" And you can reply calmly, "Well, let's discuss my experience then. I have 15 years of experience in . . ." Remember, open-ended questions are an excellent control tool in themselves.

How can you regain control of the negotiations?

- As a first step in the negotiating process, be sure to come to an agreement with your counterpart on the rules of the game, for instance, how the negotiation will be conducted.

- You could say, "What is your value if we change delivery time? How big is your benefit if . . . ?"

- Be alert and pay attention to who has the initiative.

- Take a break (call a time-out).

- Ask counterquestions. For instance, your counterpart asks, "Why do you want to change the delivery time?" Instead of saying why, you might reply, "Is that possible?"

ASKING QUESTIONS RATHER THAN MAKING STATEMENTS

Be on the alert if your counterpart refuses or evades your questions, consistently asking questions instead.

For example, you're negotiating with a venue for an event you're organizing. You ask the venue representative, "We were thinking about increasing our event size. What kind of space can you offer?" The counterpart might reply with a question: "How many people are you thinking will come?" You say, "We're thinking 200 to 300. Would you have a hall for that size?" The counterpart answers, "How would you guarantee they'll all come?"

As you can see, dialogue is still flowing and the counterpart seems open to discussion, but you never get any real data to answer your simple question.

What can you do if you find yourself dodging answers?

- Stop and review with the counterpart the rules of the game you agreed upon at the outset.

- Repeat your initial question; if necessary, point out that it wasn't really answered by what the counterpart said.

- Take a break for a discussion with your team.

KEEPING THEIR CARDS HIDDEN

While you can face a situation where you ask a question and receive another question in return, you can also be in a negotiation where you ask a question and get a vague answer. If your counterpart doesn't share any information, data, value, or cost, you have to be on your toes. You might be trying to negotiate in a collaborative way, but the counterpart is clearly in a zero-sum mindset. An easy way to identify a zero-sum negotiation is a lack of information sharing on the part of one or both parties.

Let's say you work in a bank and you're trying to get new customers to sign up for a credit card. You call a potential customer and ask, "What if we extend your line of credit and give you five times the rewards points on your first year of purchases? Would that motivate you to open a credit line with us?" Your potential customer might respond, "I don't really know" or "Mayyyybeee . . ." or "That's hard to say." Frustrating, right?

How can you get your counterpart to open up?

- Take a break for discussion with your team.

- Stop the negotiation and ask to review and summarize the initially agreed-upon rules of the game.

- Remind your counterpart that you both agreed to information-sharing (if that is the case).

- Realize you're in a zero-sum negotiation and change your strategy accordingly.

BREEZING THROUGH THE PROCESS WITHOUT BREAKING A SWEAT

You look at your watch and see that you have to leave for the airport in just 45 minutes. You still haven't addressed or settled on the most vital variable, and you are becoming quite concerned. Your counterpart, on the other hand, shows no sign of urgency and even looks relaxed.

You traveled for six hours to attend the meeting, and returning without a deal will be perceived as a failure. What you don't know is that the counterpart is equally eager to conclude the deal but has discovered your flight is leaving soon and is stalling to back you into agreeing to the best possible deal—for them. You've put yourself under the guillotine. This is just another way some negotiators put pressure on their counterpart to reach terms. And if it works, it ends up costing the opposite party a lot.

How can you cool the pressure?

- First, avoid revealing such a deadline in the first place. If your counterpart asks when your flight is departing, say something like, "Ohh, we're in no hurry. We can always rebook our flight if we don't happen to reach an agreement today."

- At the outset, come to an agreement with your counterpart on the rules of the game. This should include when and how the negotiation should conclude.

- Take a break if you discover the counterpart is stalling.

Note that a successful negotiation is not solely defined by reaching an agreement. In fact, sometimes it may be better to walk away without an agreement than to settle for a bad deal. Take your time—don't reach an agreement for agreement's sake!

I once had an alarming experience while advising a client in a negotiation. After waiting outside the conference room for hours (as an advisor I don't always participate in the negotiation, just like a football coach is not in the game), my client's team emerged, claiming to have reached an agreement with the other party. However, when I inquired about the financial details they agreed to, the head of the team had no idea and realized they still needed to work out the math. They had agreed to a deal without discussing the financial consequences. In this case, it would have been better for the team to break to discuss and come to a conclusion at another time, after they'd thought of all variables.

This incident highlights the common misconception that success in negotiation is measured solely by reaching an agreement, rather than the substance of the agreement itself. It is crucial to prioritize the quality of the agreement, rather than settling for any deal just to end negotiations. To truly succeed in negotiations, it is also essential to understand the NegoEconomics in the deal. By understanding this, negotiators can make informed decisions that benefit both parties.

For example, a supplier accepts your demand for a delivery time two weeks faster than what they originally proposed, saving you $5,000 that you would've lost by not being able to sell the product for those two weeks. However, by accelerating your delivery time, the delivery cost to the supplier is $8,000. In this scenario, instead of asking for an earlier delivery time, you would be better off negotiating for a price reduction of $7,000—you would still gain an additional value of $2,000 while saving the supplier $1,000.

PRESENTING THE INITIAL OFFER

For years, scholars of negotiation science have discussed the pros and cons of making the first offer. Despite all the discussion, they have never come to a definitive conclusion.

My take on making the first offer is this: It depends.

If you have a genuine SMARTnership with your counterpart, it doesn't matter who makes the first offer. If you are in a zero-sum negotiation, though, it can make a difference. In a SMARTnership negotiation, the rules of the game have been agreed to and the tactical use of "cheap" tricks is not required. In a zero-sum negotiation, way more techniques, some not so great, are required to "win" the negotiation. In practice, you first have to be aware of what negotiating strategy is in play (more on this in Chapter 9).

From a psychological point of view, we do know making the first offer gives you the benefit of what is called the anchor effect. This means that the first number on the table tends to act as the foundation for further discussion. If you are the one to launch a number in a negotiation, that is then the foundation for future discussion. The anchor effect in negotiation refers to the phenomenon where the first offer or piece of information presented in a negotiation serves as a reference point, or "anchor," for subsequent offers and discussions.

For example, let's say you're negotiating the price of a book with a seller. If the seller initially asks for a high price, say $50, you may be more likely to make a higher offer, say $30, even if you originally intended to offer $20. Conversely, if the seller initially asks for a lower price, say $25, you may be more likely to make a lower offer, say $15.

The anchor effect is particularly powerful when the anchor is perceived as credible or reasonable. When negotiating for a book, if the seller's initial price seems reasonable and in line with market norms, it may be difficult to push back too strongly against it. To overcome the anchor effect in negotiation, it's important to know the anchor's potential influence and to prepare alternative anchor points or counterarguments. For example, you could research similar books and their prices and use that information to make a more informed counteroffer.

What can you do if your counterpart presents the initial offer?

- If your counterpart announces an offer first, take a break to think and regroup.

- At the outset of the negotiation, when establishing the rules of the game, come to an agreement on how offers are to be handled.

- If your counterpart makes the first offer, ask questions to learn more about the offer and to help you decide how to respond.

- Do not argue. It's more productive to the negotiation to keep calm and think rationally.

SMARTnership negotiation

Zero-sum negotiation

ESSENTIAL TAKEAWAYS

- Early in your negotiation, be aware of the six signs you are losing a negotiation.

- Reduce or eliminate the argumentation and ask more open-ended questions.

- Negotiate and agree on the rules of the game.

- Use breaks when the person you are negotiating with surprises you.

- Don't accept your counterpart being in control.

Mastering Virtual
Negotiations

"Can you hear me?"

"I can't hear you!"

"Can you see my screen? I'm trying to share it."

Those are three (of many) statements we've all heard an unlimited number of times when attempting to conduct an online meeting. I did a study with World Commerce & Contracting, a nonprofit organization with 80,000 members globally, to poll 7,000 people and found that about 70 percent of commercial negotiations are conducted virtually.[1] We also learned about 41 percent of these electronic negotiations are conducted via email. Live, face-to-face negotiating is becoming less and less common as more people turn to virtual negotiating.

Despite those numbers, 96 percent of our survey respondents still felt that face-to-face meetings are superior and generate more value. I agree! When meeting face-to-face, we're able to shake hands, make eye contact, and generate some interpersonal chemistry. Not to mention, we pick up on cues that we wouldn't catch using email. A smile or a nod indicates a positive interaction; someone agreeing but furrowing their brow indicates they don't mean to agree. And we're concerned that by turning to virtual negotiating, and thereby sacrificing these factors to a greater or lesser degree, we're less effective and ultimately less successful.

It turns out this concern is quite valid. Research by Michael Morris, Janice Nadler, Terri Kurtzberg, and Leigh Thompson, published by the American Psychological Association, shows that, compared to people who negotiate face-to-face, those who negotiate online are:[2]

- Less likely to reach deals and more likely to end up at (costly) impasses

- Less likely to develop trust and more likely to *lose* trust during their interchanges

- Less likely to build significant rapport

Given all this, should we rule out conducting negotiations virtually? Of course not. They create value and achieve agreements, and combining them with face-to-face meetings not only helps boost efficiency and reduce costs—it can add something to the process.

Combinations of face-to-face meetings, phone calls, emails, and videoconferences can be great, if used intelligently. Let's look at how to do that.

EMAIL NEGOTIATIONS

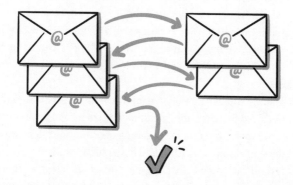

Some people fall too easily into the trap of conducting all negotiations by email. This is understandable. It's easy to schedule and conduct. It's inexpensive, especially since no travel is involved. But *be careful*—written communication has its pitfalls. It can all too easily be misinterpreted. You no doubt have some personal experience with this: being annoyed, unpleasantly surprised, angered, or even outraged by an email you've received. Or inadvertently creating such a reaction with an email you've sent.

So, when negotiating by email, be patient with your counterpart. Give that person the benefit of the doubt. Don't be quick to anger over an email that seems too brief or rude. Don't jump to conclusions about your counterpart's emotions or intentions. Take your time. Instead of arguing, ask questions.

Take care in crafting your own emails, too. Always review them before sending, taking your counterparts' viewpoint. If you were them, how would you interpret and react to what you've written?

A study conducted in the late 1960s by Albert Mehrabian, professor of psychology at UCLA, focused specifically on the communication of emotions.[3] The study found that when people communicate emotional information (i.e., feelings and attitudes), only 7 percent of the message is conveyed through words, while 38 percent is conveyed through tone of voice and 55 percent is conveyed through body language.

This study applies to emotional information. Professor Mehrabian has emphasized that his findings cannot be generalized to all communication situations and that the meaning of communication can vary widely depending on the context and individuals involved.

So, when can you use email to good effect? It's clearly a fine way to gather data, exchange facts and figures, set agendas, and establish processes. It's also a valuable tool to use before, between, and after face-to-face meetings or videoconferences. But it's unwise ever to try to resolve a conflict or disagreement by email. Such efforts are far too likely to fail since we can't read nonverbal language over email.

I believe some negotiators turn to email negotiations to avoid conflict. It's easier to come on like a tough, shrewd, aggressive negotiator when sitting behind a screen and keyboard than in a face-to-face discussion across a conference table. Still, email negotiations are not all bad. Use them when you must but be aware of their limitations. And remember, it's far easier for someone (including you!) to bluff or bend the truth in an email than in a face-to-face encounter.

It's crucial that you preserve all email exchanges related to any negotiation on a shared drive, for your own records and for internal stakeholders to access. Don't just leave them in your inbox. When engaged in confidential negotiations with external parties, do not forget the security issues inherent in email. Take care with the devices you use to access your emails, and how and where you save any attachments.

When sending attachments, make sure recipients can't see any redlined versions or comments. Use PDFs rather than Word or Power-Point documents. Unlike face-to-face negotiations, there is a complete record in emails. If there is ever a dispute, all emails related to the negotiation on your server (even if you deleted them) can be retrieved and reviewed by your line manager and legal counsel.

Take care if writing to someone of a different culture than yourself. Understand their culture: when meeting face-to-face, you can appreciate cultural differences and accommodate accordingly to ensure a successful negotiation. Those differences also exist in writing style and structure, even across departments, companies, regions, and countries.

PHONE NEGOTIATIONS

Communication studies from UCLA show that verbal communication accounts for about 38 percent of the reasons we trust someone.[4] Phone conversation is therefore clearly superior to email communication. When should you negotiate by phone?

Phone negotiation can be a reasonable substitute for a face-to-face meeting or a videoconference. But be careful—phone negotiations, like email negotiations, deny you the ability to read nonverbal cues and body language, often subtle but invaluable signals that heighten understanding and help prevent misinterpretations.

Another risk in phone negotiations is they may be requested, agreed to, and then begun quite rapidly, denying you the necessary time to prepare properly. Imagine you're sitting in your office when the phone suddenly rings. You answer and it's your colleague, who immediately says you have to do a project for your boss that she doesn't have time to complete. You're not prepared for the call let alone the intent or purpose.

During a negotiation, it is common for one party to be unprepared. This is particularly true for negotiations initiated via a phone call (or even email), since these tend to happen spontaneously. However, when you pick up a call, take a beat and take it easy. It costs nothing to be attentive to a caller and express an interest in getting back to the person when you need more time to evaluate a deal. A call remains an effective method of settling many deals. However, to make the most of a telephone negotiation, take five minutes to think your responses through.

Here's a golden rule to live by: when an opening offer is made, there is usually room for negotiation. So, whenever possible, use one of these variations to respond:

- "My thoughts weren't quite in line with that."

- "I don't think that's fair."

- "That's certainly not the best you can do."

Take a minute to rethink the situation and see if there is a better way to solve it. You will find that a little pressure often results in a better offer. If you decide to use one of the aforementioned responses, be prepared for the following response:

- "Is there anything in particular you have in mind?"

- "Sure, we can talk about this, but then you will have to . . ."

- "I'm not able to do that, but I can do this instead . . ."

If your phone rings unexpectedly with a request for a new round of negotiation, ask for a time-out. Tell your counterpart you're busy at the moment and you'll call back at some stated later time. Use that time to prepare. In negotiation, as in so many other activities, if you fail to prepare, you are preparing to fail.

Another factor to consider when starting a phone negotiation is culture and cultural differences. Different cultures impact phone communications in different ways. For example, in some cultures, a commitment over the phone is just as binding as a written agreement. However, other cultures may not view a phone agreement as carrying the same weight as a written agreement.

Finally, take care how you use your voice when negotiating by phone. Again, verbal communication accounts for some 38 percent of our reason for trusting someone. Your voice tone and inflections, speaking speed, pauses, and other vocal factors convey a wealth of information about you, your attitudes, your intentions, and your sincerity—even though the recipient may not be consciously aware of these things.

Again, phone negotiation can be a viable substitute for a face-to-face meeting, if face-to-face isn't feasible for some valid reason. But only resort to the phone if you have already established a good working relationship with your counterpart, through face-to-face or video-conference interchanges.

VIDEOCONFERENCES

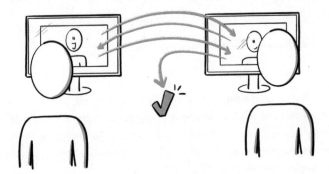

Modern technology can appear dauntingly complicated. At the same time, it offers an impressive array of valuable tools. We're able to do things considered science fiction not too long ago. We think nothing of a real-time conversation with someone on the other side of the globe, with clear sound; crisp, full-color video; and the ability to share media and graphics with just a click or two.

For the negotiator, videoconferencing is truly the next best alternative to a face-to-face encounter. It is clearly superior to email and phone negotiation, in part because it relays at least some body language, with all the information that can convey.

When preparing for a videoconference, it's important to give attention to the conferencing platform you'll use. I was recently in a negotiation in which most of the prenegotiation discussion between parties was about platform preferences. One of the parties represented a company whose policy dictated that Microsoft Teams be used. The counterpart's company policy insisted that Zoom be used, for security reasons. Before the first actual negotiation meeting could begin, the parties spent an enormous amount of time hashing over platform choice.

Another important factor is ensuring the chosen technology is actually working reliably. Make sure you've installed any software updates to your computer and the app you're using for your videoconference. Check your Wi-Fi settings and be sure you have a strong internet connection. This can involve considerable back-and-forth between parties (and sometimes their in-house technical people), including testing and retesting. I have experienced far too many instances of delayed, interrupted, and otherwise mangled negotiations, all because of glitches and breakdowns of equipment, software troubles, faulty or unreliable internet connections, bandwidth inadequacies, and the like. And I bet you have too! Again, careful setup and adequate testing by all parties is crucial. Even then, there are no guarantees—but at least you'll have a far better chance of a smooth meeting, unmarred by technical woes.

As for the negotiation itself, approach a videoconference as if it were a face-to-face meeting. Just bear in mind that, because of the limitations mentioned, even the best online encounter is inherently more challenging than a face-to-face one. Online meetings typically have to be shorter than live ones, due to technical limitations. You have to be mindful of the need for breaks. The schedule must be firmly set and agreed upon; the same goes for the structure of the negotiation.

Videoconferencing is a remarkable advance over email and phone, in terms of interpersonal dynamics. So don't underestimate the importance of small talk as a means of building rapport when videoconferencing.

Finally, even if you're doing the bulk of your external negotiations online, you can still have in-person internal negotiations, planning meetings, and so on. The in-person meeting is still king.

WHAT TO REMEMBER WHEN NEGOTIATING VIRTUALLY

Regardless of whether you'll be negotiating in person or by phone, email, or video, you must know the rules of the game—*how* you're going to approach the negotiation itself. You and the other party need to discuss and agree on that as a first order of business.

Perhaps the most basic element in our rules of the game is the negotiating strategy to be followed. Will we take a zero-sum approach or a collaborative approach, aiming for SMARTnership? If we choose the SMARTnership approach, we'll also need to agree on how to go about it. Who will start? While formal turn-taking is not strictly necessary, try to keep offers and counteroffers well defined and in sequence. Speak up if it's unclear whose "turn" it is.

Be aware of and careful about making assumptions about the other's interests, intentions, offers, proposals, or conduct. Less face-to-face interaction means each side has less information about the other, so the chance of incorrect assumptions—and the trouble they can cause—is greater. No one needs that kind of trouble. So, take care, maintain communication, and ask clarifying questions.

BE CAREFUL WHAT YOU DO ONLINE

I don't recommend negotiating on social media platforms and consider it unwise to conduct a serious negotiation on Facebook, Twitter, WhatsApp, or similar social platforms. Similarly, don't be continually but randomly switching between texts, emails, phone calls, and videoconferences. Agree with your counterpart on a negotiating structure and plan—which formats will be used at which stages of the process or under different potential circumstances—and then stick to your agreement.

Finally, please remember that when you are negotiating in writing, everything is being recorded and stored. In face-to-face meetings, this will not be the case—unless someone records and preserves the proceedings. If this is not done, neither party is at all likely to completely and accurately recall everything said, and the context in which it was said. That can lead to some very messy and expensive consequences. So be careful not to make unwise statements or commitments that could later be used against you.

In a virtual negotiation it may be easier to attempt unethical tactics because facts presented by one party are harder for the other to verify. Resist the temptation. The consequences are just as severe—perhaps more so—due to the incriminating evidence created when virtual negotiations are automatically archived.

ChatGPT AS A NEGOTIATION TOOL

People often ask if I would recommend using ChatGPT and other artificial intelligence (AI) tools as a negotiation advisor. My simple answer is yes! I find ChatGPT and similar tools offer a structure and support often superior to what the average human negotiator is capable of.

I conducted a study with World Commerce & Contracting where we arranged three different negotiation scenarios with two groups:

Scenario 1: Group A versus Group B

Scenario 2: Group A versus Group B using ChatGPT

Scenario 3: Group A using ChatGPT versus Group B using ChatGPT

They all received the same simulation: two hours to prepare as a team of two individuals and then 30 minutes to conduct the negotiation with the counterpart. Despite having the exact same time to prepare and conduct the negotiation, the outcome was quite different.

What did we find?

Scenario 1: Group A Versus Group B

Humans do as humans do. We talk a lot—often about stuff that isn't relevant. It's in our nature to try to create rapport. In this scenario, the negotiators went off the prepared script, discussing options not mentioned in the simulation until they finally ran out of time without reaching an agreement. Both teams weren't particularly open with details that mattered to the negotiation, and sharing data was limited.

Scenario 2: Group A Versus Group B Using ChatGPT

Compared to scenario 1, this negotiation was more structured since ChatGPT was involved. Group B ended up having clearer data and calculations using ChatGPT, which was able to assist with identifying the negotiable variables, running the calculations, and preparing questions. The parties reached a result just in time.

Scenario 3: Group A Using ChatGPT Versus Group B Using ChatGPT

Compared to the previous two scenarios, this one concluded the fastest. They closed the deal, negotiating variables that ended in benefitting both parties, in good time before the deadline.

USING ChatGPT IN EACH STAGE OF NEGOTIATIONS

ChatGPT can be a helpful tool for brainstorming negotiation strategies, providing information about the negotiation subject, and assisting in crafting persuasive arguments. The following tips will help you use it effectively.

Preparation

- **Research the subject matter:** Begin by asking ChatGPT questions about the topic you're negotiating. Gather relevant data, industry insights, and any other pertinent information to help you make informed decisions during the negotiation.

- **Set your objectives:** Clearly define your goals and expectations, and ask ChatGPT to provide suggestions for potential trade-offs and alternatives you can offer during the negotiation process.

- **Identify your NBA (next best alternative):** Ask ChatGPT to help you brainstorm your best alternative if the negotiation fails. Knowing your NBA will give you a stronger position to negotiate from.

- **Define the scenario:** Clearly outline the negotiation context, including the parties involved as well as their goals, interests, and constraints. This information will help set the stage for the simulation.

Strategy Development

- **Develop your negotiation strategy:** Use ChatGPT to brainstorm possible negotiation tactics and strategies, including your opening offer, target price or terms, and any concessions you're willing to make.

- **Analyze the other party:** Ask ChatGPT about the counterpart's interests, concerns, and potential negotiation tactics. This information will help you understand their perspective and prepare for possible objections.

- **Plan your communication:** Request suggestions from ChatGPT on how to frame your arguments, build rapport with the other party, and effectively address any objections or concerns they may have.

- **Set up communication:** You can interact with ChatGPT via the OpenAI API. For real-time or multiparty negotiations, consider using a platform that allows simultaneous communication among participants, such as a chatroom or messaging app, with ChatGPT integrated into the platform.

During the Negotiation

- **Use ChatGPT as a real-time advisor:** While engaged in the negotiation, ask ChatGPT for advice on how to respond to the other party's proposals, objections, or tactics. ChatGPT can help you find creative solutions and maintain a productive dialogue.

- **Provide context:** To ensure that ChatGPT understands the scenario and its role, start the conversation by providing a brief summary of the negotiation scenario, the parties involved, and any relevant background information.

- **Manage emotions:** If emotions become a factor in the negotiation, consult with ChatGPT on how to address them and maintain a constructive environment.

- **Assign roles to ChatGPT and the human participants:** You can either use ChatGPT as a negotiation partner, or as an assistant providing advice and strategies during the negotiation.

- **Engage in the simulation:** Begin the negotiation by asking questions, making proposals, or expressing concerns. As you interact with ChatGPT, it will respond according to its assigned role. If it's acting as a negotiation partner, it will engage with you in a simulated negotiation. If it's acting as an assistant, it will provide you with advice, strategies, or relevant information.

- **Monitor and adjust:** Continuously assess the performance of ChatGPT during the simulation. If it provides irrelevant or incorrect information, gently correct it and restate your request. You can also use prompts to guide the AI toward a desired outcome or to refocus the conversation.

Review and Reflect

- **Postnegotiation analysis:** After the negotiation, ask ChatGPT to help you analyze the outcome, identify areas of improvement, and develop strategies for future negotiations.

- **Debrief and reflect:** After the negotiation simulation, take some time to reflect on the experience. Analyze the interactions, responses, and outcomes. Identify areas of improvement and consider how the AI can be better utilized in future simulations.

INPUTTING INFORMATION INTO ChatGPT

Remember that ChatGPT is an AI language model and not specifically designed for negotiations. It may not fully grasp complex negotiation strategies or concepts. However, it can still be a useful tool for practicing communication and negotiation skills, especially in a low-stakes environment.

The way you address the system is vital for the quality of the outcome. Upload the information you have available and ask questions like: What would be the negotiation strategy based on the information? What questions should I ask my counterpart to learn more about their priorities? General questions yield general answers. Ask about specific activities you are planning (such as inquiring about the other party's parameters) and use that as inspiration. Use "How can" questions instead of "Can." For example, ask: How can we make a maximum price of $1,000 work? Don't ask: Can DK Logistics accept $1,000?

ChatGPT can assist with concrete negotiation variables and do so very well. But it is not great at defining what the room for negotiation is in any deal, as it doesn't have access to both parties' cost and benefits.

Remember to add new information to the thread with something like: My counterpart has now agreed to XYZ. Write information and parameters down in text format so it can be quickly copied and pasted.

Ultimately, AI tools like ChatGPT can be a valuable asset for negotiators who want to improve their communication and negotiation skills. By leveraging the power of AI, negotiators can gain a deeper understanding of the negotiation subject, develop more effective negotiation strategies, and achieve more positive outcomes.

GENERATING VALUE

We know that in a virtual negotiation, creating extra value is more difficult than in a face-to-face exchange. So, in a virtual negotiation, take the time and care to focus even more closely on generating value than you might when working face-to-face.

Too often online negotiators attempt to blindside the other party by smacking down an opening offer too early. Yes, it's absolutely true that there is a "first-mover" advantage in negotiating: the person who makes the first offer usually prevails. But this should not prompt you to shove a term sheet into the virtual hands of your counterpart before you've even said hello.

Instead, plan your opening offer carefully, but resist presenting it until at least two things have happened. First, greet the other party and ideally even schmooze a little. Second, discuss with the counterparty how best to use their time. Indeed, research indicates that "late" first offers—those presented only after appropriate pleasantries are exchanged and the proverbial table is set—are more effective than first offers made earlier on.[5] So by all means, craft your opening offer beforehand, but don't be in a mad rush. Wait for the optimal moment to reveal it.

Just as you would in a face-to-face negotiation, make good use of breaks. When needed, take time-outs to think things through. This is fully acceptable and expected. Virtual negotiation is here to stay. So, approach it with an awareness of the challenges it presents, and keep the principles and tips here firmly in mind.

ESSENTIAL TAKEAWAYS

- When negotiating over email, don't make assumptions about the other party's meaning—ask questions when something doesn't seem clear. Avoid misinterpreting.

- Treat phone negotiation as a useful supplement to face-to-face meetings and videoconferences.

- Even if the bulk of a negotiation will be virtual, take steps to create a face-to-face relationship before actual negotiations begin.

- Pick the channel (face-to-face, videoconference, voice, email, etc.) that will be most effective for putting all relevant information and detail on the table.

- Work to develop a personal negotiation style (collaboration, competition, etc.) that's a good fit with the communication channel you are using.

- ChatGPT and other AI can be useful tools in building your negotiation strategy.

Conducting
Negotiations Abroad

It seems clear that when traveling to Korea from the United States, we experience a different culture. But leaving your company's headquarters, crossing the street, and entering a different company's offices can also be a cultural shock. Culture is many things. It's meeting the opposite gender, a representative from another region of the same country, or even someone from a different part of the same city. Culture is meeting an individual from another company or a different university. You meet different cultures every day, so even if you don't negotiate internationally, this chapter is important.

Whether traveling abroad for fun or business, read everything you can about the country you're visiting in order to better understand foreign cultures and become aware of your own prejudices about them. From slender pamphlets to extensive tomes, novels, newspapers, weeklies, and trade journals, the reading material is endless. If you can't find the material yourself, turn to the Ministry for Foreign Affairs or the Export Council of the country you're visiting. The internet is obviously another excellent source of information, including government websites on almost any city in the world.

You can also attend special classroom or online courses on foreign cultures, both at home and in other countries. In a few days, you'll get a good overview of the history and culture, and you'll meet people who can provide even more information. Don't forget that there'll always be colleagues in other companies and organizations who have been there before you. Try to tap their knowledge.

It requires extensive preparation to truly understand a culture other than your own, let alone to negotiate with someone from another culture. Since each negotiation is unique, it requires special attention. Let's talk about some of the factors requiring special attention in international negotiations.

INTERPERSONAL CHEMISTRY

Whether a decision is made or not in a negotiation often depends more on whether there is a personal chemistry between the parties than on measurable factors like price and performance. This is even more true in international negotiations than in negotiations at home. It's easier to be rational (less emotional) when negotiating within familiar frames of reference. Time and time again internationally experienced negotiators stress the importance of personal relations. People want to know whom they're doing business with. They want to meet the people they've dealt with before, people whom they trust and on whose word they rely. This is where socializing enters the picture, and here it will be determined if the interpersonal chemistry works out.

Socializing is regulated by written and unwritten rules entrenched in the culture in question. A small mistake on your part can, at worst, be seen as an indication you're impossible to work with, and at best, be seen as an understandable faux pas for a foreign visitor. For example, not participating in dinner in some cultures may be offensive. Similarly, not presenting your business card with two hands can be a faux pas in some Asian cultures.

In some countries the old rules governing social behavior have been watered down over the years. Tradition means more in some cultures than others. In Japan, the ancient, also known as "sado" or "chado," is a traditional art of preparing and serving tea with a focus on aesthetics and mindfulness. But anyone observing this old norm today runs the risk of being perceived as a fossil. Making that sort of social faux pas in American culture rarely leads to a deal falling through— Americans won't stop the deal if they are handed a business card with one hand instead of two. That being said, etiquette, or how we behave and conduct ourselves around others, has seen a revival in the United States and Europe.

CLOTHING

A CEO from a Nordic company is receiving businesspeople from a South American company. The CEO brings a young new employee into the meeting as a way to give her more experience in negotiation. To his surprise, the CEO discovers the South American businesspeople are far keener to listen to the young employee than to himself. In the end he has the distinct impression he's being ignored by the South Americans. Why? The way he dresses! The CEO is wearing a casual blazer with a colorful shirt and jeans, while the young woman is wearing a dark linen suit and an expensive-looking watch. Their respective suits send a signal about which of the two has the higher status.

Why are clothes important? The way you dress is part of your language. It's impossible to put on something without at the same time sending various messages about your social status or background, what you do for a living, which level your job is, how successful you are, or even your personality and mood.

You can also show you accept the norms existing in a country by following their dress code. Some international travelers openly demonstrate their disdain for these norms by intentionally breaking the code—for instance, by wearing sneakers and a T-shirt to an international negotiation. They may do this to show they are free and independent, not tied down to society or class expectations. Others might unknowingly break the code by not researching enough before arrival. That being said, it is possible that old rules of etiquette have simply been replaced with new, unwritten, and perhaps even more stringent rules. A dark suit can be replaced by jeans, a T-shirt under a jacket, and sneakers. And that's OK if both sides of the table are comfortable with the new norm.

If you depart from the dress code, you run the risk of having the other party misunderstand you. You might not think it necessary to wear a tie and cuff links to the meeting, but your counterparts might take it as an insult that you didn't bother to be presentable. They might not know if the reason you're underdressed is faulty knowledge about the business dress code of the country or if you're doing it on purpose to show you're above tradition. Trust is a keyword in negotiations. If you want the other party to listen to you and understand your message, behave in a manner that inspires confidence, including dressing the part.

CULTURAL DIFFERENCES

Too many negotiators have told me their transactions failed because they weren't aware of cultural differences between their culture and the culture of the country they were negotiating in. Traveling the world doesn't mean much if you don't walk away with some understanding of that culture. Before negotiating abroad, ask yourself what you know about that culture. If the answer is "not much," then do some research! You may find some vast differences between your culture and theirs— hold your judgment. Do your due diligence when working internationally so that you are aware of the culture, customs, and traditions of your counterparts and be mindful not to do anything that may be considered offensive. However, that doesn't mean compromising your own values or your company's. If something in another culture goes against your values or your company's values, find a way to stick to yours while being respectful of the differing values. After all, who's to say your culture is superior to another's?

MEALS

Food, drink, table manners, time, place, and rituals are things you must learn about when conducting a lunch or dinner business meeting abroad. Most of us know that people in some religions and cultures don't eat pork or drink alcohol, but do you know:

- Where you're not supposed to arrive on time for dinner plans?

- Where bringing a gift to your meeting host is important?

- Where it is considered rude to finish your plate, or leave food on your plate?

- Where business talk during a meal is taboo?

- How extensive a meal has to be?

In Denmark, an efficiency- and cost-conscious country, people might easily ask business partners to have lunch in the company cafeteria. Both the environment and the quality of the food may be unfamiliar, perhaps even shocking, to some foreigners. Foreign visitors might be unaccustomed to Danish customs and misunderstand the purpose of the meal. Whereas the Danish think of meeting for lunch to discuss business as time efficient, to a foreign visitor the meal might have great social importance. Some cultures use a meal as a way to get to know one another over the course of two or three hours. They offer the very best food and etiquette they have as a way to show their guests they're honored and respected. A simple white bread and cheese sandwich, followed by a cake wrapped in plastic, might be easily misunderstood by someone from a culture where visitors are treated to full course meals. Retiring to an affordable and sensible Holiday Inn for the night, after dinner at the most folksy restaurant in town, isn't likely to improve matters.

Learning about your counterpart's culture may be the difference between sharing a meal that seals the deal or having that person feel mistreated.

PUNCTUALITY

Just like socializing, punctuality is an important factor in negotiations abroad. Many cultures view punctuality in different ways. A businessperson from a culture where time efficiency and planning are the norms might be thrown off by arriving in a country where the culture is to take your time and go with the flow. Germans are known for their punctuality and can find offense in even a few minutes' delay. When out of your element, you are more likely to make mistakes or even concessions in negotiation. For example, if your counterpart abroad is taking their time and you're more used to rigid timetables, you might try to speed up the pace of the negotiation by making concessions. Avoid that temptation. You'll attain a less satisfactory result than if you had just adjusted to the other party's timetable.

Some cultures are in such a hurry when negotiating, as well as socializing, that they attempt to finalize the negotiations even before the other party realizes they've begun! One of the countries with the fastest paces is the United States. Americans make such fast decisions that it has led to the expression "postbusiness negotiations": negotiations that are held after a negotiation is over in order to clear up all the headlong agreements.

SMALL TALK

For socializing to function well, a precondition is to have something to speak about. But sometimes talking shop may be breaking a taboo, depending on where you are. Small talk is difficult for many negotiators. It's hard for them to speak of themselves, or their country, or their counterparts' lives and country, for hours and hours before getting to a subject in which both parties are interested. Those negotiators might even speak of technical matters to avoid having to touch on the human aspects of life.

I've come across many negotiators who are socially awkward. They have no ability to speak of anything but the job, technical matters, and, in some cases, sports, irrespective of whether they're speaking to their colleagues or business partners. For those who need help with small talk, practice is key. Some common small talk questions:

- "Are you married?"

- "What does your spouse do for a living?"

- "Do you have any children? How many?"

- "How old are your children?"

- "Where do you live?"

- "How far is your commute?"

Bring a picture of your family, your house, your boat. Talk a little about your own country. Read the other party's newspapers, trade journals, and weekly press so you can ask questions about current events. Try to get as much information as possible about the other party's interests. And, when in doubt, talk about the weather.

As a side note, religion and politics are obvious minefields—especially if the religious and political systems are very different from your own. Remember, you're not in the country to offer your personal assessments of the society you meet. You're there to do business. It's best to avoid the topics of religion and politics entirely; redirect the conversation if your religion or politics is brought up.

NEGOTIATING IN A FOREIGN LANGUAGE

Sharing a language is very often a prerequisite for socializing. It's possible, but difficult to communicate through an interpreter. In a perfect world, you would know one or more languages other than your own. But sometimes it isn't enough to speak a foreign language. Your negotiation language, like the lingo you use in negotiation, might be a foreign language to the other party, causing an increase in communication breakdown.

It's often said that to really understand a culture, you need to embrace the full language of that culture, including its body language. Body language isn't universal. A survey of typical gestures, like the OK and thumbs-up signs, shows that these occur normally in a majority of countries, but that their meanings differ greatly. Gestures that in our part of the world have a positive context may be an insult in other countries. Gestures meaning yes in one country may mean no in another. Showing the wrong gesture in another country can lead to serious confrontation.

Certain gestures can be ambiguous.

To what extent should you learn some phrases in the other party's language? Should you insist that all parties use a common language? For instance, someone who is in business with German and French people could set the common language to English, even if they all speak the three languages.

INDIVIDUAL VERSUS GROUP CULTURES

Group cultures and individual cultures are two different ways of understanding and organizing social behavior within a community.

In group cultures, the focus is on the collective well-being of the group over the individual. Group cultures tend to value interdependence, harmony, and conformity to social norms and values. People in group cultures often prioritize maintaining social harmony and avoiding conflict and may place a strong emphasis on traditions and rituals that reinforce a sense of shared identity.

On the other hand, individual cultures place greater emphasis on personal autonomy, self-expression, and independence. In individual cultures, people tend to prioritize their own goals and interests over those of the group and may be more likely to challenge or question established norms and traditions. In individual cultures, personal achievement and success are often highly valued, and competition and individual achievement are typically seen as positive traits.

It's important to note that these cultural dimensions are not mutually exclusive and that many cultures can exhibit elements of both group and individual cultures to varying degrees. Additionally, the emphasis on group or individual values may vary across different domains of life, such as family, work, or leisure, and can also shift over time as societies and individuals change.

TITLES AND SENIORITY

In most Western cultures, it would sound unnatural to address people by all their titles and names. But in some cultures, it's essential to show respect when addressing someone. In some cultures, using an individual's last name and title is the only acceptable way to address the person. In Germany, for example, you would address your counterpart by title and last name: Dr. Mueller, as opposed to his first name Fredrick (or, worse, Fred). In Japan, you would add the honorific suffix "-san" after a person's family name. But in some cases, Japanese businesspeople may use the honorific with the person's first name if Western: Paul-san instead of just Paul. High social position acquired through inheritance or education means that a great deal of respect will be shown in many countries.

BUSINESS PRACTICES

Business practices and legislation in foreign countries may be completely different from our own. For example, some places don't accept complaints as a valid reason for a refund. In some others, earning a commission on a sale is not allowed. And in others, if you're building a hotel abroad, local staff are required to do part of the work. The costs involved in this may be considerable. You have to pay a higher salary and perhaps even a commission to an agent.

Sometimes a handshake and a short written statement of the guidelines agreed to will suffice for a lengthy collaboration to work. Other times an extensive, detailed contract will be required. And in some cases, if the collaboration doesn't end up working, another party can question the written agreement and its validity. Trust is important when dealing with different negotiation styles.

Consider any differences in how a foreign country might conduct financials. What are the requirements and conditions for payment, do you have access to foreign exchange (and at what rate), and is authorization from the Central Bank or another authority needed before payment can be affected? In China, for example, a buyer must open a confirmed, irrevocable transfer and divisible letter of credit approved by the Bank of China. What does it mean? That the bank of the importer guarantees payment provided the documentation meets the contract provisions. The buyer can't hold back payment for any reason, and the Bank of China can use payment directly, in part or in full, to pay for other transactions. This is very different compared to many other countries, where there might be no requirement of a letter of credit or the transaction is simply done between the two organizations' own banks with the use of the national bank of the country.

Always consult local legal experts before venturing into unknown markets. Lawyers can give you valuable advice before and during the negotiations. Make sure that any dispute concerning the interpretation of contract provisions can be settled under your country's law. For financial reasons you may be forced to accept an unsatisfactory settlement because you can't wait on an arbitration proceeding, which could be lengthy and costly. Make sure that arbitration will ensure quick decisions.

Any agreements should also be written in a language you know, for obvious reasons. Don't accept a translation from the original text into English, as things may be lost in translation. Familiarize yourself with the standard contracts that foreign organizations, authorities, and companies use well in advance. Take a look at what other companies in a similar situation have done for guidance—you'll avoid some unpleasant surprises and you'll get a better understanding of what can be negotiated and what you should be on your guard against.

Once you've put your signature to a document, there isn't much a lawyer can do to help you. Never forget that your best possibilities to negotiate are before you've signed.

FORMAL CONTACT PATHS

Before stepping into a negotiation, carefully examine what the decision-making process looks like and what decisions, authorizations, and personal contacts you should have. If you're doing business with a public authority in a foreign country, don't expect they'll automatically inform you of everything you need to know. If, for instance, you need a work permit to carry out installation work abroad as a foreigner, this may turn out to be very costly. Familiarize yourself with the decision-making process of the foreign company you're working with. Who are the stakeholders of the enterprise and what sort of power do they have?

TECHNICAL COMPETENCE

Sometimes you may need to train the other party's staff, give operation warranties for the machines, or use workers that are not your own for installation jobs. From the start, you must rely on the skills of the staff in that other country. Despite guarantees issued by the other party that they are technically skilled, know English, can read a blueprint, and have many years of experience, you may be in for serious problems if you don't familiarize yourself with the training differences of the country in question.

For example, you're working with foreign staff that have arrived in your country to get special training in operating buses and trucks. You realize their licenses from their home country don't qualify them for a training license in yours. Or they don't speak the language, even though their company insists they know enough to get by and figure out road signs. It's not easy to get an idea of the work level and pace of foreign staff, if it varies greatly from the work level and pace in your country. There might be differences in training in both countries, or even instructions or other things that get lost in translation. Nor is it always enough to use knowledge tests to pinpoint these issues, as knowledge varies greatly throughout nations.

A group of officers came to the United States from another country to participate in a military training course, but first they had to undergo a test in mathematics so that the US supplier could check if they had the necessary qualifications. All but one passed the test. He was very offended. Unfortunately, he had the highest rank in the group. On the following day he left for home taking the whole group with him. It would have been a better solution first to have held a meeting with the group to work through any potential work pace and communication problems. It's important to be discreet and sensitive and avoid stating that the purpose of the meeting is to evaluate the competence level of the staff. You're not evaluating competence—you're evaluating differences in order to make sure everyone is on the same page.

DEALING WITH OTHER TECHNICAL STANDARDS

The norms we base ourselves on when comparing offers and proposed solutions vary a great deal from one culture to another. In Nordic countries, the culture is to think of solutions in an efficient, productive, and quality-focused way. As such, Nordic businesspeople might assume their choices are generally the correct choice, since they function with the thought that the highest quality is the best quality. When negotiating with people from countries where other priorities take place, they might find it hard if they're not open to other ways of doing things.

DECISION-MAKING

Discrepancies in the decision-making process often explain why negotiations seem to drag out interminably. In some cultures, decision-making is delegated to those with the higher job title or experience. American salespeople on an assignment abroad often have wide discretionary powers when it comes to making decisions. But when they go home, they find they have to explain their every decision to someone higher up.

Let's compare this with the Japanese system. In Japan, a complete consultation is required in advance of any decision with all the individuals who will be affected by the decision. Decision-making is considered a very serious matter, and the Japanese prefer spending time ensuring that everyone understands what's at stake. Every executive affected must seek confirmation and advice from his or her employees. A negotiation may take a long time as a result of this decision-making process. The counterproposal you receive back is the result of what the executive group has agreed. Trying to force an early decision won't work.

CORRUPTION

Under European and US law, any kind of bribe is illegal. However, in certain countries, bribes are the rule rather than the exception. The authorities acknowledge that bribes actually exist, and expenses for bribes are tax-deductible for the enterprise, provided the expense can be documented. Bribes constitute a difficult problem both in moral and practical respects. We can't simply apply our own values to condemn bribes abroad; conditions in other countries may be completely different from our domestic ones. And there have been many corruption scandals in which people and companies in European countries and the United States have been involved. When conducting negotiations abroad, always follow your company's code of conduct regarding accepting gifts, and never be pressured to accept something that could get you in legal trouble at home.

• • •

When hosting visitors from a different country and culture, there are sometimes decisions to be made about how much to share and to which extent you should try to protect them against cultural shock. Never go so far as to edit out everything that might seem strange or foreign to visitors by offering them a sterile international environment. Visitors like to get to know something about your country and everyday life. Humans are inherently curious and experiencing a different culture inspires a lot of curiosity. But think about what can be misinterpreted within your culture and how much you can forgive a visitor not knowing about your culture.

But you may think, *Shouldn't the other party adjust to the culture they encounter? Aren't we all responsible for learning about a country before we go there?* As visitors, we let the host show the way. After all, who knows better about their own culture and country than the host? On our own home turf, we often hide ourselves. Maybe we even take it for granted that the other party is familiar with our customs. If you are open, positive, and receptive to taking the first step and teaching your visitors about your culture, you'll get a positive response and build goodwill. In turn, your visitor will be comfortable and confident doing business with you.

ESSENTIAL TAKEAWAYS

- Before traveling abroad to conduct negotiations, learn about the culture you're about to meet.

- Be aware that a culture clash could be the reason an agreement isn't successful.

- Culture is not only traveling to another country. A culture clash could occur when you meet someone from another company in the same country.

- Negotiation language isn't just your ability to speak a foreign language—be mindful of body language as well.

THE ESSENTIALS APPLIED

Negotiation Competence Self-Assessment

Now that you understand the essentials, you're ready to *apply* the essentials. To get started, complete the benchmark assessment below. Your answers will help highlight the areas you can target in Part II to make the most dramatic improvement in your negotiations. No one else needs to see this, so feel free to be brutally honest.

Directions: Please read each statement and use the following scale to indicate how strongly you agree with it. Then add up the rating column for a total score at the bottom.

1 = Never
2 = Rarely
3 = Sometimes
4 = Usually
5 = Always

Rating	
	You are usually well prepared for negotiations.
	You view a negotiation as a collaborative process.
	If you concluded a negotiation that turns out to be negative for the other party, you accept a renegotiation.
	You take the time to really listen to the other party while negotiating.
	You build and/or work in a team in your negotiations.

	You try to find alternate values you can gain from a negotiation.
	You are not argumentative in negotiations.
	You focus on establishing and improving trust before and during negotiations.
	You discuss ground rules with the other party before negotiations start.
	You build an agenda for negotiation meetings.
	You take breaks during negotiations.
	You establish clear roles and responsibilities within your negotiation team.
	You don't concede points without getting anything in return in a negotiation.
	You enjoy negotiating.
	You can identify the other party's behavior in most situations.
	You use some form of negotiation planning tool.
	You don't view negotiation as a win/loss situation.
	You generally ask questions instead of arguing.
	You always know when you're entering into a negotiation.
	You take the initiative in your negotiations.
	Maximum score: 100

Add up your total score to determine your percentage of the 100 possible points. This score is only the "starting line"—a way to help measure your progress as you keep learn more about negotiation in this Part, "The Essentials Applied." Once you've had a chance to practice your new negotiation tools and strategies, repeat the assessment to track your growth.

Right now, this benchmark assessment can also help you gain some valuable insights into your specific negotiation skill level. Any statements that you ranked 4 or 5 may represent your strengths. Statements that you ranked as 1, 2, or 3 provide you with opportunities for improvement.

Circle or highlight the three to five statements with the lowest scores. As you work through Part II and begin to practice some of your negotiation skills in real time, pay close attention to those specific areas. If you focus on accelerating those particular skills, you'll likely see the biggest change in your negotiation performance and results.

The Phases of Negotiation: Prenegotiation

Many moons ago, I worked with a chairman on my board who often liked to say, "Imagine all the time we save by not preparing!" I wouldn't agree with my former chairman's approach. To negotiate successfully, it is essential to understand the various steps involved in the process.

In my experience as a negotiator, I've identified all the different ways a negotiation works, including common negotiation pitfalls and mistakes negotiators make as well as constructive strategies for overcoming them. I discovered 10 phases that make up a negotiation, which can then be divided into three stages, which I will talk about in the next three chapters: prenegotiation, negotiation, and postnegotiation. In prenegotiation, we spot a negotiation opportunity and then prepare for it. During negotiation, we open the negotiations, make our arguments, identify all our options, and then bargain for a deal. And in postnegotiation, we close and sign the deal, run a postmortem of how the negotiations went, and decide if we will continue the business relationship into future negotiations.

As you read through each phase and start comparing your experience with mine, you'll encounter some "aha" moments. These phases are not always experienced in the same order, and some negotiations may not involve all 10 phases. However, recognizing and understanding these phases can significantly improve your negotiation skills and increase your chances of success.

I divided the negotiation process into 10 distinct steps for the purpose of this book, but in reality, it is impossible to identify all 10 steps in *every* negotiation. Often, one step seeps into another and makes negotiation a continuous process. It is not uncommon for parties involved in negotiations to make an offer and immediately begin bargaining when they find themselves in a negotiation situation. We may not even realize we're negotiating until the end of phases four through seven, or sometimes, we only realize we're negotiating once there is a conclusion.

With that in mind, let's dive into prenegotiation.

PHASE 1: SPOTTING A NEGOTIATION

Your phone rings and the caller opens with, "I was wondering if we could move that shipment up a week." And with that, whether you recognize it or not, a negotiation is underway. Things of this sort happen all the time—and they aren't limited to business situations. As previously mentioned, I've identified that as much as 80 percent of your communications with others can be categorized as negotiations. Every time an individual in a conversation tries to persuade another person about something, they're in a form of negotiation.

There are many ways a negotiation can arise in your everyday professional or personal life:

- A client requests a price quote.

- You are presenting a new piece of work to an art gallerist for a potential showcase.

- City representatives gather at a town hall to discuss the construction of a new overpass over your road.

- The requirements of a project you were working on have changed and you have to figure out how to adapt.

- You submit a draft budget to your boss, but she rejects it.

From these examples, it's evident that negotiations can occur voluntarily or under pressure. The choice to continue or end a voluntary negotiation is entirely up to you. The only exception to this is when it comes to disputes and complaints pertaining to a contract violation. Regardless of any personal opinions regarding legal contracts, you must abide by any you've signed.

It's easy to recognize a formal negotiation. You and the party you're negotiating with agree to meet on Thursday at 1 p.m. at your office and negotiate a price on services offered. But even before an agreement to meet is reached, there may well be a number of emails, phone calls, or other communications, each one of which involves a negotiation: What day is most convenient to meet? What time? Should you meet at your office, theirs, or a neutral spot? These small negotiations ultimately lead to a large-scale, formally scheduled one.

The most dangerous negotiation you'll ever get into is the one you don't recognize as a negotiation. Imagine you're sitting at breakfast when your spouse asks, "Honey, are you going to be in the office all day?" "Yes," you answer. "I've got a huge project I need to finish and introduce to my manager, so I be staying until that's done." Your spouse replies, "Great! Then you won't be needing the car. I need it, so would you be a dear and take a cab to work? I'll see you tonight. Love you."

In this situation, you didn't realize it when your spouse launched a negotiation. As it continued, you didn't recognize it for what it was. When it was over, you didn't spot it as a negotiating loss. In phase 1 of most negotiations—spotting a negotiation—is critical for your success.

Listen and watch for the following openings. They are often disguised as something else, but in reality, each marks the start of a negotiation:

- "We have to . . ."

- "I need you to . . ."

- "I think we . . ."

- "We/you should . . ."

- "Let's think about this . . ."

- "How do we . . .?"

- "What do you think about . . ."

- "Here's what we need to do: . . ."

- "How can I help you?"

Each time you encounter one of these openings, pause for a moment. Take a breath before you reply. If you've been asked a question, consider whether you should reply with a counterquestion, such as, "Why do you ask?" "Would there be a financial benefit for you if we . . .?" "Will there be any cost associated with changing . . .?" You get the idea.

The "small talk" prior to the actual negotiation contains a lot of negotiation in itself: "How is business going for you guys?" "Are you impacted by the supply chain issues?" Often this laid-back conversation reveals an enormous amount of valuable information if we handle it correctly, since we don't consider small talk to be a part of actual negotiation.

PHASE 2: PREPARING FOR A NEGOTIATION

I enter a carpet shop in Istanbul, Turkey, and ask to see a particular carpet a friend told me he'd seen there. The shop owner greets me but doesn't go to find the carpet at once and try to sell it to me. Instead, he invites me to sit and offers me a drink. He was about to have tea himself and my company would be welcome. I accept. We sit, and the owner's assistant begins preparing our tea, boiling the water and meticulously measuring out the right amount of tea for each cup. I'm fascinated by the little ceremony as the shop owner explains the proper method for making Turkish tea. In doing so, he establishes good rapport with me and gains my trust.

As our conversation progresses and our tea is served, the owner obtains more information about me:

"How long have you been in Istanbul?"

"How long do you plan to stay?"

"Where have you come from, and where will you be going next?"

"Where are you staying?"

"Have you visited the bazaar before?"

I tell him that I've been in Istanbul for four days, that I'm staying at the Hilton, and that I've come from Bulgaria and will be going on to Yugoslavia the following day. I've not been to the bazaar but have visited other tourist attractions in the city.

He warns me against pickpockets, and I check that my money is still in my pocket.

The owner wasn't just making conversation. He now knows that he has before him a customer who has little time and much money; one who hasn't spent a lot of time bargaining in the bazaar. Yet he needs to know more about me before negotiations can begin.

He asks his assistant to bring the carpet I've inquired about. While the assistant is away, the owner asks if I would mind seeing a few other carpets. I agree, and he takes me a bit farther into the shop, where three carpets are spread out on the floor. He asks how I like them, and my comments immediately reveal that my knowledge of carpets is limited. I remark on the carpets' colors and patterns and mention that one of the three is a popular style back home. The owner asks how much such a carpet would cost in my country. I reply, "$4,000 to $5,000."

Soon the assistant appears with the carpet I've asked about, and negotiations begin. Through our conversation, the owner armed himself with all the information he needed to steer the negotiation forward to a conclusion. Because of all the information he gathered before the carpet even appeared, he was able to start the negotiation on a strong foot.

There is an old negotiating maxim: Not preparing is the same as preparing for a failure. The purpose of preparation is to increase your flexibility in a negotiation—which in turn enhances your ability to meet the challenges that will almost inevitably arise. When you ask questions, gain a sense for your counterpart's goals and interests in the negotiation, and consider their perspective, you can build a negotiation that ultimately meets both your needs and goals.

Prepare for the Unexpected

Negotiations tend to take on a life of their own. Unexpected factors arise, creating unanticipated problems, but also opportunities (if you know how to recognize them). Negotiation isn't a completely rational process, where the two parties' reactions can always be predicted. You might walk into a negotiation in a calm state of mind, only to walk out upset that the other party tried to take the upper hand and the negotiation didn't go as you planned in your mind.

Preparation doesn't mean working out an extremely detailed plan where you try to predict how every little interaction will go. Preparation is meant to provide you with a map—a tool for staying on course and getting your bearings when the unexpected arises. It's meant to provide some security, an overview of the possibilities, obstacles, and alternative routes.

With good preparation you can map the route or routes toward your goal clearly, depending on what you know and what you're able to reliably predict. When negotiations begin, your objective should not necessarily be to arrive at your goal by the shortest possible route. You will surely need more information about the other party's situation, their requirements, the needs behind those requirements, alternatives they might be open to, their degree of flexibility, how changes in terms and conditions would affect them, and so on. Given all this, it is generally well worth taking the time to learn as much as you can.

As part of this process, you have to open your own emotional channels and be sensitive to what you see and hear. Your ability to interpret psychological interactions between people, and how you consciously and subconsciously react to those, helps you define, approach, and achieve your goals. You'll need to be flexible when new obstacles and opportunities arise that cause you to revise your plan.

Also, be aware of time pressure. If you try to enter a negotiation with a deadline, it is important to leave yourself enough time to prepare. You don't want to leave money on the table by rushing through a deal just to meet a deadline, and you most definitely don't want to arrive to that deal uninformed and frazzled. If there's a deadline and you need more time, you can always add in a deadline extension as part of your negotiation. If that's not possible, then during the negotiation, focus on listening to the other party's terms and avoid making final decisions on the spot.

If you fail to prepare in advance, or fail to analyze an ongoing negotiation, you might find yourself in a stressful fight-or-flight situation. My ancestors, the Vikings, were arguably some of the most fearsome warriors of medieval Northern Europe. Yet even they had a choice when facing an enemy—freeze or draw a sword and fight. Luckily for me, the choice was often the latter! Like the Vikings, a modern negotiator faces a fight-or-flight response when caught in a stressful negotiation, whether it be because of lack of preparation or factors like lack of trust in the opposing party. Stay calm and clearheaded to avoid giving that other party the upper hand.

Create an Agenda

A meeting agenda is one of the best tools you can use to prepare for a negotiation. It allows you to set the tone for the negotiation and keeps you from straying from the main goal. Setting an agenda can help tighten a negotiation and create structure, which can help increase your confidence in your negotiation tactics. However, don't be too strict with your agenda—if there's some unexpected sidetracking from your agenda, that's OK. You can always find a way to get back on track. Be flexible, make sure you understand the situation, and pay attention to what the other side expects from you.

An agenda is also tactical in nature. You decide which issues should be discussed in what order based on the agenda you present. If the other party sets the agenda, pay attention to the expectations for how the meeting will go. This can ultimately help you shape your argument

AGENDA

- Hello and welcome
- Negotiation strategy
- Splitting NegoEconomics
- Variables
- Value created
- Conclusion

and further your goals. I can't stress enough how preparing an agenda will help you succeed in any negotiation. It allows you to avoid surprises and walk into the room with confidence.

Add Checklists to Your Negotiation Toolkit

Checklists can be extremely useful tools when preparing for a negotiation, but be wary of using them to follow a single formula. Every negotiation is different, so build and adjust a checklist as needed based on each individual negotiation you engage in. Build a checklist after you've done the prep work for a negotiation so that you know what to add to it.

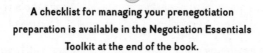

A checklist for managing your prenegotiation preparation is available in the Negotiation Essentials Toolkit at the end of the book.

Use your checklist to remind yourself of actions, ideas, facts, and insights that have led you to successful negotiations in the past. It can help you spot any areas you may have overlooked or given insufficient attention to when preparing, understand any difficulties you encountered in the course of the negotiation, and highlight constructive moves you and your counterpart came up with to reach a successful conclusion.

Create a Negotiation Planner

Another valuable tool in any negotiation is your negotiation planner. This chart shows you different possible outcomes in any particular negotiation. It prepares you in case your negotiation isn't going the way you want. If you reach a standstill on your goal, what are you willing to concede? Where are you willing to compromise to reach your goal? If you haven't prepared ahead of time for bargaining, you'll end up making concessions that negatively impact you.

Your chart should have the following for both your own negotiation goals and your negotiating counterpart's goals:

- **Variables:** These are the terms you are negotiating, which can include things like price, delivery dates, conditions of payment, or terms for a promotion.

- **Starting point:** This is where you are starting in your negotiations. This will include specific details about your goals and desired outcomes for your end of the negotiation.

- **Negotiating space:** This lets you know where you have wiggle room in your negotiation. If the negotiating counterpart pushes back, where do you have room to meet them halfway? This gives you an idea of how flexible you can be, and the alternatives you can take advantage of.

- **Changing of conditions:** What is the outcome if you need to compromise on your goal? This reveals the points that are sensitive for you, and what the consequences are if you give in, hold fast, or compromise.

Here's an example of what that would look like in a negotiation between a client and a manufacturer:

Starting Point	Negotiation Space	Changing of Conditions	Variable	Negotiation Space	Changing of Conditions	Have in Mind/ Competitor
$520,000	$490,000	-$30,000	Price			Avoid concession
January 6th	February 10th	10,000/week	Delivery Date			What is the cost to the client?
2 years	1 year	+$45,000	Warranty			
Net cash		Internal interest rate 12%	Payment Conditions			Remember to ask questions

Your negotiation goals   Your counterpart's negotiation goals

Filling out your side of the chart is the easier part, but how do you know what your counterpart's goals are before a negotiation? Either you can research how your counterpart has negotiated past deals or you can create many different scenarios on how a negotiation would go on their end.

Fill out this planner with an open mind. What would it look like to give in on certain points? And if you have to give in, what can you get out of the negotiation instead? Being open to finding agreement terms other than the ones you originally wanted creates confidence because ultimately you'll be in control of which variables you can and cannot compromise on. But beware of revealing too much—only reveal flexibility where you absolutely must.

Asking things like "How much would you save if we could . . ." opens a door to possibilities that wouldn't have originally been on the table if you hadn't been willing to find a beneficial solution for both parties. It also opens room to discover your negotiating counterpart's flexibility on their terms, which benefits you as well. Being willing to compromise and, more importantly, knowing what you're willing to compromise on, will give you the upper hand and set you up for success. A conversation might go like this:

> Sure, I can be open to a longer delivery time. It might entail some extra expenses, but I think it would still be worth your while. Of course, delivering as early as you can gives you a leg up over other suppliers we are talking with as we compare our options. How can we come to a delivery date that benefits both of us?

It's hard to know how flexible another party will be in the negotiating room, and it can be even more difficult to determine the consequences of a possible change in original negotiating terms. You could compromise on the delivery date, but would that affect your inventory down the line? One of the main objectives in preparing for a negotiation must be to fill out your negotiation planner as much as possible. Be sure to think about how you can ask questions in the room without revealing too much of your desired outcome too soon. If you do reveal too much, you end up losing some of your negotiation power.

Research the Other Party's Customs

Gathering information about the other party, such as their values or customs, helps you anticipate how a negotiation will go. Recall from Chapter 5 that different countries have their own customs and traditions, and it is important to know those going into a negotiation with an individual or company from a foreign country.

Some years ago, I met a European company owner who had been involved in a business negotiation in an Arab country. The negotiation was in its final phase, and the European negotiator was convinced an agreement was imminent. Suddenly, he felt the Arab negotiator pat him on the leg under the negotiating table—a gesture that signified they were in agreement and everything was good. This custom doesn't exist in Europe or North America, and the European misinterpreted the gesture as an inappropriate advance. Outraged, he got up from the table at once and announced he was returning to his hotel. Had the European taken some time to study the local culture, he would have come away with a handsome deal instead of an embarrassing disappointment.

Preparation is the be-all and end-all of success when it comes to negotiation. Nevertheless, I routinely come across negotiators who are ill-prepared. A common excuse is lack of time. But my experience is that many people who enter a negotiation haven't constructively utilized the time available. They've failed to familiarize themselves with the other party's style and values, locked themselves into a certain approach, failed to research the roles of the people on the other side, or haven't considered enough possible alternatives, to name a few common mistakes. Don't limit your preparations to practical matters only—reserving tickets and booking hotels; compiling a list of negotiation documents; and gathering blueprints, queries, and letters. If you fail to get a clear overview of the negotiation ahead, and get hung up on small details instead of assembling a roadmap for your negotiation, you lose.

Be Open to Other Points of View

As part of the negotiating seminars I hold, participants are tasked with preparing and executing a few mock negotiations. Having discussed matters for a few hours within their groups, most participants feel they're well prepared. However, when the mock negotiations are over and analyzed, participants often discover they've failed to consider negotiations from the other party's point of view, leading to losing out on a deal.

Let's consider this example: a Swedish bus manufacturer received an inquiry from China about purchasing technology for building a bus manufacturing plant. The Swedes were convinced the Chinese were short of industrial experience and, therefore, incapable of building buses for at least a decade. So instead of providing what the Chinese had requested, the Swedes offered them ready-made buses. The Chinese explained that no, they did not want ready-made buses, they were in the market for the technology. Understanding the Swedes' doubts, they invited them to send a delegation to China to see for themselves that they had the capacity to use the technology.

Following their visit to China, the Swedes were more convinced than ever that the Chinese weren't currently capable of building buses.

They invited the Chinese to send a delegation to Sweden to demonstrate their most up-to-date products. The Swedes offered to sell them ready-made "building blocks," which the Chinese could assemble into complete buses.

Having seen these components, the Chinese objected, saying they had a different kind of bus in mind. They showed the Swedes blueprints of the bus they wanted. The Swedes found it difficult to keep straight faces. "But that belongs in a museum," they said. "We haven't built buses like that for 20 years. No one in his right mind would build a factory for those today!"

Having reached a standstill, the Chinese ended up negotiating a lucrative contract with a German enterprise that offered them exactly what they needed and wanted: the technology to build 20-year-old vintage buses. The Germans wisely viewed the negotiation from the other party's point of view and adjusted their offer to the prospective buyers' requirements and resources. The older-style buses might not be wanted in Europe, but they perfectly suited the needs and resources of the Chinese.

Learn from Experience

When you've completed a negotiation, take time to look back on your road map and compare it to what actually occurred during the negotiation. Most likely you'll find errors or omissions in your preparation, showing you how you could have avoided negative outcomes. Analyze all your negotiations to learn how to recognize what communication methods work best. Did the other party respond well to your pushback? Or could you have spent more time listening and finding more common ground? Analyze the signals you were getting from the other party. Were they firm or frazzled or confident? And how did you respond to those signals? This postmortem on your negotiation is an excellent way to improve your negotiating skills. Make it a firm habit to set aside time for a calm and measured analysis. Your future negotiations depend on it.

ESSENTIAL TAKEAWAYS

- Listen carefully for any signal that tells you that you're about to get into a negotiation.

- Preparation is essential for your success in negotiation, even for the seasoned negotiator.

- Learn to recognize who has leverage in a potential negotiation.

- Use checklists to prepare your side of the negotiation, and use the negotiation planner to create structure for your negotiation.

- Always start a negotiation with variables you believe might generate value for both sides.

CHAPTER

7

The Phases of Negotiation: Negotiation

PHASE 3: OPENING NEGOTIATIONS

There are several challenges to overcome when you begin negotiations of any kind. How to open a negotiation is one of them. Consider the following statements and questions:

> "Your products are too expensive. Would it be possible to get a lower price from you?"

> "I really need that budget on my desk by tomorrow."

> "Why should I go with you and not your competitor?"

> "Please find attached all our requirements. Send us your new offer as soon as possible."

> "This is my final offer."

What would you do if you entered a negotiation and heard those right off the bat? Probably get frazzled—why *should* you go with my offer and not my competitor's? Stay calm, remember your prep work. Ask questions before making any decisions.

For a fruitful negotiation, it is important to understand where the other party is coming from. Insist on knowing what they want and don't view their demands or threats as risks and costs, but rather as opportunities and signals. Assess the situation and their statements. "Why should I go with you and not your competitor?" Just think to yourself, *They could go to my competitor if they wanted to, but they're here negotiating with me. Why is that?*

Make sure to pay attention and listen to what the other party has to say. You won't lose anything by merely listening. When you have enough knowledge and information at your disposal, you'll be able to negotiate more effectively. Listening does not mean you agree with everything the other party says. Nor should you abandon your viewpoint. And if the other party listens to your comments without stating any objections, don't assume they are in agreement. Silence during a negotiation isn't equivalent to consent.

If the other party starts the negotiation before you do, let them set out all their requirements up front. If you make a better offer too soon, you might lose more than you wanted to. Before you submit a completely new offer, see if you can counterbid their offer. Otherwise, you'll end up giving up all your gains as you make concession after concession. Refrain from being hasty during this phase. Instead, take a cautious, hesitant approach. This will help you gauge what the other party hopes to gain from the negotiation before you make decisions.

Amicable openings are extremely important as they set the tone and the groundwork for the negotiations. To create a constructive climate and generate good cooperation, get to know and learn to trust each other during this phase. While it's important to have good interpersonal chemistry, there are situations where this isn't possible. Some negotiators prefer a combative approach. By making you feel uncomfortable, they attempt to stress you out or paralyze you to gain the upper hand. You may feel insecure as a result of their aggressive opening. To ensure a constructive and positive outcome, steer the other party away from combativeness if at all possible (otherwise, you may have to respond with combativeness as well—more on how to respond to combative behavior in Chapter 9).

To build an interpersonal relationship with someone as you enter a negotiation, it's essential you learn about them, establish trust with them, and help them relax and feel at ease. Share a meal—after all, an empty stomach is not an appropriate condition for negotiating, according to ancient Chinese wisdom. As my wife always tells our sons, "You have to wait until he eats before you talk to him! Otherwise you'll just be frustrated."

It's also a good idea to share something about yourself with one another. Talk about the last concert you went to or that latest show everyone is watching; enjoy each other's company. When in doubt, talk about the weather. An experienced diplomat once told me that to be an effective diplomat, you need to be good at two things: talking as much as possible about the weather and knowing when to be silent.

Building interpersonal relationships can be challenging for some people. Some negotiators find the negotiation process frustrating when dealing with a variety of business partners. Establishing rapport with new people may be particularly difficult for those who do not frequently interact with strangers in their daily work. In international negotiations, socializing is far more prevalent, which could cause problems for those who cannot create good chemistry with strangers. No matter which country you come from, people will enjoy doing business with you if you are likable. The way we do business with each other goes far beyond technical issues, presentations, and finances. It is about personal connection, comfort, and chemistry.

When discussing the weather, for example, what is the appropriate amount of time before they start to think you've lost all interest in negotiating? That varies from negotiation to negotiation. Sometimes, if you know your counterpart well, you can conclude the small talk phase within a few minutes. However, as it happens in some cultures where talking about the weather is all the rage, the process may be stretched out to several weeks. Be mindful of cultural norms when taking negotiation meetings internationally: You may be committing a faux pas by getting down to business right away, essentially shutting down negotiations entirely. That's something many negotiators have learned the hard way!

Some negotiators expect the other party to jump right into a sales pitch after just a few opening platitudes. "Yeah, yeah, it's sunny out—so what kind of gains can we expect to see in the next quarter?" For a negotiator trying to take some time and build rapport, it can be jarring to have to cut to the chase. This can put you in a losing situation, if you're not ready for it. How should you react in this situation? You could jump to presenting the basics of your negotiation pitch and shutting up. This way, you let the other negotiator fill the space by talking, possibly allowing you to gain some valuable information you otherwise wouldn't have gotten if you got flustered and continued on and on with your pitch.

PHASE 4: HANDLING ARGUMENTATION

Argumentation in this phase means anywhere from your general arguments in a negotiation (e.g., "As you know, I've been a good tenant this past year and always pay on time, so I believe I deserve some leeway on a rent increase.") to actual combative arguments (e.g., "Your prices are ridiculous, you need to come down some!"). Negotiating opponents test their strength against one another when they use these types of arguments. Arguments that are well-crafted and credible may help a party win the upper hand and avoid concessions. Consider this argument:

> I compared your quote with quotes from other companies, and it looks like the other companies can provide what we want as well as you can. We are surprised at your high pricing. Is your price quote possibly inaccurate?

What does the buyer hope to accomplish with this argument? He's testing the company to see if they'll lower their prices. He's not sure whether or not what they've offered is a good deal, or if it's just an initial offer that can be negotiated. The last thing he wants to do is pay more than he has to. Other suppliers, he says, can offer much lower prices because they are on an equal footing. Maybe it's true, or maybe he's bluffing—he is being very vague, after all. He doesn't detail how those competitors offer a better service, doesn't define by how much their services are cheaper, or doesn't explain why he suspects a mistake in the quote. It's often difficult to tell the difference between reality and a bluff. By mentioning the possibility of miscalculation, he gives them an opportunity to adjust the price without making it obvious that they are overcharging him. He's giving the company an opportunity to save face.

Don't Cave to Pressure

In some cases, as in the one just described, negotiators attempt to pressure the other party into making concessions. Don't cave to the pressure, otherwise you risk looking insecure and vulnerable. And worse, you risk losing a lot in the deal. In a unilateral concession, one party in the negotiation room gives up a lot more and doesn't get anything in return.

To reach a better negotiated solution, the discussion should be open and constructive. Seeking clarification is very important in getting as much information as possible so you don't leave money on the table in a negotiation. During the negotiation, the goal is to find the NegoEconomics (i.e., alternative solutions that increase how much you get out of each concession). For example, when a seller offers to shorten her delivery time, and her costs are less than the buyer's profits, she is engaging in NegoEconomics when the parties are transparent and know each other's costs and profits. NegoEconomics occurs when the customer's benefit exceeds the supplier's cost.

In general, if you take the initiative to negotiate first, you're in a better position to make and win your case, since you can lay out the agreeable terms before the other party does. However, this may not always be possible. Sometimes, the other party takes the initiative. In such instances, don't be hasty; you don't need to hurry to reach a conclusion and make your decision. Even if you are well-acquainted with the negotiation process, it is best to take it easy so you don't stress yourself out. Before acting on the next step, take a moment to think things through.

To understand the importance of taking a beat to gather your thoughts, consider the following situation. During a telephone conversation, a salesperson attempts to offer his customer a surplus shipment of memory modules (RAM). He claims to sell at a 15 percent discount compared to normal prices:

> **Salesperson:** Our company has obtained a shipment of RAM EDO 32Gb. If you purchase at least 100 units, you will receive a 15 percent discount off the regular price.

> **Customer:** I'd like to know more about that since we use a lot of RAM, specifically EDO 32GB. Could we speak later? I'm not sure how much we can take.

> **Salesperson:** I'll wait here while you find out.

> **Customer:** Just a moment while I check inventory and speak with the department.

The customer returns a few minutes later to order 300 units, and he is satisfied with the purchase. But could he have gotten a better deal?

Let's explore how this could have gone differently:

> **Salesperson:** Our company has obtained a shipment of RAM EDO 32Gb. If you purchase at least 100 units, you will receive a 15 percent discount off the regular price.

> **Customer:** What an intriguing proposition. If I purchase more than 100 units, would a higher discount apply?

> **Salesperson:** We might be able to give you a deeper discount. How many were you planning to purchase?

Customer: I'll get back to you in half an hour. I have an important meeting now. It might be worth considering what price you can offer for a 500-unit order while you are waiting.

Although there is no meeting to attend, the customer wanted to consider the proposal without feeling rushed. He is aware that to negotiate this deal successfully and seamlessly, a backup plan is necessary. So he starts investigating how the price compares to that of other suppliers. When he contacts another supplier, he gets a similar price. He quickly learns that RAM is abundant on the market. After he gathers enough information, he calls the original seller:

Customer: What kind of discount can you give me on 500 units?

Salesperson: A discount of 18 percent is yours if you order 500 units.

Customer: RAM is pretty abundant right now, but a better price might make me more inclined to buy now.

Salesperson: How about an additional 1 percent?

Customer: OK, 19 percent is all right. But I will not be able to take more than 300 units in that case.

Salesperson: I think we've reached an agreement.

In this particular example, the customer tests boundaries and gets a better deal, all without being rushed. During this process, he took a beat to acquire information, assess the situation, set a goal, and pursue it. He was also careful to not react negatively to the small discount increase and ensured that there was no damage done to their supplier relationship, while still managing to save some money. Although the first offer he received was good, he did not accept it immediately. As far as he was concerned, there was room for negotiation.

Negotiate from a Position of Balance

The dialogue in a negotiation should be balanced. When the opposing negotiator is expressing their points, just sit and listen. Avoid interrupting, even if they argue something you know to be false, otherwise you're just devolving into combat mode and not gaining anything from the interaction. Imagine you are sitting with your son. You're asking him if he did his homework. He starts explaining that due to his obligations to play soccer he wasn't able to finish the homework. Don't interrupt but let him finish before engaging in further discussions. This way he feels like he has said his piece and you're not just ganging up on him because you are the adult.

The difference between an argument and a demand is important to note. Claiming something is too expensive, for example, is not necessarily a demand. It could also mean that the negotiator is looking for an explanation on why that price is worth it. In order to understand what the other party wants, you must get more information, instead of assuming and going on the defensive. You can counter with: "What would make this pricing worth it to you?" It is important that you get concrete counterproposals in order to understand your actual standing and what you agree on. Never assume what the other party wants or likes.

Be careful not to make decisions based on just one argument. Listen for all demands and objections from the other party in order to make an informed decision. Obtain as much information as possible before making a decision to accommodate the other party. It is your responsibility to stick to the boundaries you have set for yourself when deciding whether to accommodate unexpected demands. But *do not give away* anything without *receiving something* in exchange. Always get something in return when you concede a point. When listening to the other side of the negotiation, consider these questions:

> Are there any consequences for you if you follow these demands?

> If so, what are the best solutions to avoid those?

> Are there any demands you should make in return?

> And how could these benefit the other party (as well as yourself) in order to sweeten the deal?

It's useful to take a break to analyze the answers you've obtained by listening. It also allows the other side to assess your proposal as well and figure out what they can offer to reach a compromise.

On the flipside, the arguments (and counterarguments) you make may need to be repeated and clarified to ensure the other party understands your proposal. Consider illustrating and substantiating them visually, if you can. Make accurate claims, and don't exaggerate your offerings. You also obtain credibility when you provide solid evidence for your claims. How much will it cost and why? Write out the math. Show your negotiation counterpart that you know your stuff, and that in turn shows your worth.

PHASE 5: IDENTIFYING YOUR OPTIONS FOR NEGOTIATION

When two parties are deadlocked in a negotiation, one must concede some points in order to move forward—a deadlock benefits no one. The negotiators must be more open to other ideas or specific in their arguments in order to achieve their desired outcome.

For example, a seller is offering 10,000 pounds of bricks at $10 per pound. You could say, "That's too expensive!" But making a counteroffer is a better idea: "$8.75 per pound is the maximum we can pay." Now that the seller has a level to work from, he can glean a better understanding of how to proceed with negotiations.

An offer for $8.75 is $1.25 below what the seller is offering, since the original price of $10 is based on a consignment of 10,000 pounds. Let's say the seller's threshold of pain is $9 per pound. What happens next? There are two potential solutions to this problem:

1. **In order to keep the customer happy, the seller lowers his price.**

    The seller could make a unilateral compromise—a compromise where there is no expectation of getting something in return. This transaction resembles those common in Turkish bazaars:

    Seller: I think $9.75 is a good compromise.

    Buyer: Those numbers aren't good enough; you can do better.

    Seller: If you place your order today, I can reduce another 25 cents.

Buyer: There is a difference of 75 cents between my demand and your offer. Assuming that we split the difference, we come up with $9.10. That's my best estimate.

Seller: Deal!

As you see, the seller didn't try to get more. In fact, the seller was very accommodating by offering another 25-cent reduction in a matter of minutes without first exploring alternatives. But the seller is still getting above the $9 per pound threshold of pain, so he is negotiating within his limits. That means he is not actually compromising—in order to reach a genuine compromise, *both* parties would have to give up something, not just the seller. A situation like the one just described often involves counterbids to induce concessions from the other party.

Remember that opening offers are usually only the first offers used as a launching point to the true discussion. My extensive research reveals a general formula you can use to figure out the other negotiating party's true threshold of pain: divide the difference between the bids by two, divide *that* figure by two, and then subtract it from the original amount. So a negotiator who counters with $500 when you want $1,000 has a threshold of pain of $875:

Difference of $500/2 = $250, divided by 2
= $125 and $1,000 − $125 = $875

So knowing that, you could start with 1,000, counter their 500 offer with 955, then 875, and so on and so forth until you stop before their actual threshold number. The idea is to keep even figures to a minimum so you don't end up losing more than you should. Taking big leads in a negotiation only leaves room for more loss than gain. Reduce the percentage to 9.25 percent rather than going from 10 percent to 9 percent. Slow and steady wins the race, after all. When you are negotiating nonnumerical variables, the same rule of thumb applies. The first offer is most often negotiable.

2. **The seller offers a larger quantity.**

Here, the seller asks the customer to take a bigger amount of product, with the intention of evening out the price. Here's how that goes:

> **Seller:** I could give you a better price if you take more than 10,000 pounds.

> **Buyer:** OK. How many pounds are we talking about?

> **Seller:** How about 15,000?

> **Buyer:** That could work. What kind of pricing would I get on that?

> **Seller:** If you buy 15,000 pounds, I could reduce the price to $9 a pound.

> **Buyer:** That $9 a pound sounds good; we'll discuss quantity later. You paying for delivery is what I would really like. It is not possible for us to pay $150 per ton. There is no doubt that your competitors pay for delivery.

> **Seller:** But will you take 15,000 pounds still?

Buyer: The freight cost on that sounds expensive. That's a lot of pounds and potentially a lot of shipments. We'll have to think about it. What could you offer for all that?

Seller: We can possibly deliver in one go.

Buyer: If you could plan a single delivery to eliminate freight charges, that would be great. And $9 per pound sounds great. As soon as I know the quantity we'll need, I'll let you know.

Seller: OK, I'll be waiting for your call.

Here, the seller ended up offering an excessive amount of concessions, which is obviously a no-no. He started off well enough, making an enticing offer by saying he could reduce his price if the buyer agreed to buy more inventory. Can you pinpoint where things started to go wrong? The buyer took the opportunity to stand tough and steer the negotiation in her favor when the seller offered up $9 per pound as his price. But the buyer didn't leave a whole lot of room for silence, you say. How should the seller have handled this? He could have countered with:

Seller: If you take 15,000 pounds, I'll see if I can reduce the price.

See how that's different? This way, the seller gives himself some time while he waits for the customer to respond. The seller must only allow for a concession once he is certain that the customer is comfortable with the quantity increase. Another concession should be demanded: "Can you accept 500-pound packages instead of 50-pound ones?" By doing this, he signals that taking and giving are prerequisites for changing the offer.

Signals Versus Arguments

Sending signals is a way negotiators can emphasize other solutions and open up room for negotiation. A signal contains a specific message, while an argument is often composed of standard platitudes that are difficult to interpret. While signals help locate openings, argument is used to establish and test positions of strength.

Arguments

- "The price is too high."

- "The price here is the lowest we have ever offered."

- "Other companies offer more for lower prices."

- "We can work something out."

Signals

- "The highest I'm willing to go is $8.75 per pound. How can we get to that price?"

- "This is the lowest price we can offer for the quantity requested." (Notice the tone: the seller is hinting at a different price depending on the quantity requested.)

- "Your competitor is offering $9 per pound for 13,000 and discounting the delivery fee if we order an additional 2,000. Can you match that?" (The buyer has to do some research to get real quotes from other sellers.)

- "We can throw in free three-day shipping if you order 15,000 at $9 per pound."

Using signals can help a negotiation move forward, but it's very common to miss signals the other party sends. Factors contributing to this include:

- Uncertainty or insecurity

- Poor listening skills

- Being close-minded to openings offered by the other party

- Being on the defensive

If your negotiation is riddled with signals, it is very important to observe whether the other party understands what you're saying. Request a summary of your proposals from the other party. Writing them out on paper or a whiteboard, if available, is a good idea. Put the other party on the spot by demanding a position: "How do you feel about my suggestions?"

Negotiators, especially on the purchasing side, prefer to wait until the other party opens up before speaking. Some even believe that sending signals is wrong. They feel that if they do this, the other party will have it too easy, which leads to argumentation. That's an easy way to get stuck in a stalemate! Consider using the following signals in your next negotiation:

- "Should you entrust us with the responsibility to supply everything you need, we are able to . . ."

- "If you prefer to pay with cash, you can always/we can offer . . ."

- "If you are flexible with delivery times, we will be able to . . ."

- "We would appreciate your help in making it possible for us to . . ."

Sometimes, your signals may be quite evident and yet, other parties pretend to not see them. If they ignore signals they can stall for time, and if there's a deadline to reach a deal they could use that to pressure you into more concessions.

A negotiator can also use silence to draw out a concession. The following scenario illustrates this:

> You get a job offer and you are negotiating the position salary with HR. After citing all the reasons why you're worth higher pay, you say, "I think a 20 percent increase in salary is commensurate with my experience." The HR generalist stays silent for an uncomfortable (to you, at least) amount of time, so in your need to end the silence and in fear of losing the offer, you say, "But I can be OK with 5 or 10 percent above the offering salary." The HR jumps on that: "Great, we can do 5 percent more. Welcome to the company, I'll send out your contract for you to sign shortly." You just got lowballed! A better strategy would have been to ride out the silence and give the HR generalist a chance to at the very least say, "I'll speak to the hiring manager and see what we can offer."

PHASE 6: BARGAINING

By this phase, you've already presented your desired terms and made your arguments. Now it's time to propose an offer and discuss the price or other details.

Part of negotiating inevitably means finding compromises and concessions. However, you do not have to accommodate every demand made by the other party. Some may not even be negotiable to you. You are allowed to reject any proposal detrimental to what you want from the negotiation. Remember, rejecting a proposal doesn't necessarily mean the negotiation is over. Find another value that could be negotiated instead. For example, how much is it worth to the other party if you shorten the delivery time without asking for more money? Does that person expect to receive payment more quickly? Questions like these may help to negotiate a better deal than you initially anticipated.

Making unilateral concessions or accepting any old offer are the two biggest mistakes people make in purchasing negotiations. Let's say a furniture salesperson says she can authorize a 10 percent price reduction on a mattress, but a customer is demanding 12 percent. The salesperson accepts immediately. Suspicious, right? That's because the salesperson was actually allowed to offer 15 percent off, but the customer was hasty in their negotiation and missed out on an extra 3 percent. Maybe the customer wasn't comfortable with pushing back, thinking he was getting a good deal already with 10 percent off. Either way, you're not going to get the best deal if you take the first offer. Conversely, if you're the one making the first offer, make sure that you do not throw your best offer out first. Instead, try testing the waters. Remember the formula for your threshold of pain from Phase 4 and only raise or lower your offer incrementally.

When navigating the various negotiation options, both parties must have agreed on principles that should be carried forward past the negotiation meeting. Don't be ambiguous! Be as clear as possible on the terms you are seeking. Instead of saying, "Maybe I could reduce my price on this item, what are you thinking?" say, "I can give you a 10 percent discount if you buy five items."

Remember the other party must be able to fulfill their end of the bargain, so make sure that's possible by setting realistic terms based on what you've learned about their goals so far in the negotiation. Note that you should postpone any negotiation until you know the other party is ready to move forward and that the person you are dealing with has the authority to carry out the transaction.

By putting the other party's terms and your proposed solution on the table, you can lock them in before you conclude the deal. "Can we reach an agreement if I find a solution that will provide you with . . .?" By doing so, you'll be able to determine how far you need to go and what routes are feasible for you to take. Don't fall into the trap of sending mixed or weak signals: An overly generous concession from a seller could lead a buyer to believe the seller has more room to bargain than they actually do.

In most cases, it's better to make your offer comprehensive, covering all details of the agreement. A package deal is the best option. The alternative is creating a salami negotiation where each point is discussed until they are all clarified.

The Salami Negotiation

Salami negotiation is a technique used in negotiations where the negotiator breaks down a complex issue into smaller, more manageable parts, like slicing a whole salami into smaller rounds. This allows the negotiator to approach each part of the issue with more focus and clarity, making it easier to identify and resolve any issues that may arise.

You can use this technique in a wide range of negotiation scenarios, including business deals, personal conflicts, and even writing projects. In business deals, the negotiator can divide the deal into separate parts, such as price, delivery time, and payment terms, and negotiate each part separately. This approach makes it easier to identify any issues with each part of the deal and reach a mutually acceptable agreement, but it increases the risk that the counterpart loses track of what has been negotiated.

In personal conflicts, salami negotiation is used to break down the issue into smaller parts, allowing the parties to work through each part separately. This approach helps to prevent the negotiation from becoming heated or confrontational, as the parties can focus on one specific issue at a time.

In writing projects, salami negotiation can be applied by breaking down a complex topic or chapter into smaller sections or subtopics. By focusing on one section at a time, the writer can make steady progress and avoid feeling overwhelmed by the task of writing an entire chapter or book. Each section becomes a mini-negotiation, and once each section is complete, the book comes together cohesively.

The benefits of salami negotiation are numerous. First, it helps to identify and resolve issues within the individual parts of the negotiation, leading to a more successful outcome. Second, it helps to prevent the negotiation from becoming heated or confrontational, as each part is approached separately. Finally, it makes the negotiation more manageable and less overwhelming, allowing the negotiator to make steady progress and reach a mutually acceptable agreement. However, the technique can be abused as well if one party in the negotiation is the only one slicing the negotiation and trying to eat each slice.

Negative Example of a Salami Negotiation

In a zero-sum negotiation you can benefit from using the salami technique, but it's not recommended in collaborative negotiations.

Salami negotiations could begin with a discussion of minor cost points. As an example, a negotiator might try to squeeze the transportation costs in a delivery negotiation first. As long as the cost in question isn't prohibitive, the seller will easily cave in. Further payment conditions may be demanded by the negotiator, alleging that the seller's competitors offer similar terms. If these concessions fall within the seller's negotiation limits, the negotiator could give in, hoping that his concessions will be sufficient to conclude the sale. However, he cannot be sure whether his concessions are sufficient. He hasn't tried to lock in the seller and was instead focused on making the seller put all his demands on the table.

Next, the negotiator is concerned about the price of the goods themselves. After much discussion, the negotiator gets to a price he's comfortable with. But despite all the seller has offered, the negotiator adds to his list of demands a free case of spare parts. There is no way the seller can meet that demand, as he cannot afford it. This is the negotiator's last demand, which squeezes the seller, who feels like he can't turn down this order. By breaking down each point, the negotiator has managed to get what he wants out of the seller.

Are You Negotiating or Haggling?

I recently read a story about a father who was proudly explaining how he'd been teaching his son to negotiate. The father's account went like this:

> The other day, my son asked if he could have a few chocolate chips.
>
> I said sure, you can have 10.
>
> He asked for 20.
>
> I upped my offer to 12.
>
> He lowered his request to 18.
>
> I made a final offer of 15, which he accepted.

The reason I mention this story is because it explains how negotiation is perceived by many people. In a nutshell, they think of negotiation as a process wherein one party wins by coming away with more of some resource, while the other comes away with less. But is such a scenario actually a negotiation, or is it merely haggling?

The father's example is what could loosely be called a positional negotiation, or "zero-sum," in which one negotiating party ends up with more and the other with less. Let's say there was a total of 20 chips in the bag. That means there was a fixed number of chips available on the negotiation table. The son isn't able to end up with *more* than 20 (what was available to him to begin with), and the father wouldn't end up with his son having none (try telling your kid they can have none of the tantalizing sweets in front of them—I bet you'll get some resistance, to say the least!). Both parties begin with a proposal favorable to themselves, and both seek to maximize their own gain and reduce their pain. The son wanted all 20 chips to satisfy his sugar craving; the father knew he would have to deal with his son's sugar high if he didn't limit him to 10. But how could the son satisfy his craving with only 10?! Eighteen chips would do as a counteroffer. Father and son make concessions back and forth until they reach an agreement, which happens to be right in the middle between their two opening offers. People often find such a compromise to be a good solution in a negotiation. But, in most cases, it actually is not.

What should have happened instead is collaborative negotiation, which is quite a different style. Here the two parties seek to expand the kinds and quantities of resources on the table. Rather than looking at just one resource (the 20 chocolate chips), they consider a range of additional factors. In real-world negotiations, additional factors might include durations, warranties, delivery dates, and even certainties. Collaborative negotiation requires the parties to change their mindsets about what negotiation is and what it isn't. They need to be willing to exchange information, be more transparent, question wants and motives, and learn more about each other's interests. In a zero-sum negotiation, the parties are more likely to hide such considerations for fear that they will be used against them. The level of trust present is almost inevitably much lower in zero-sum versus collaborative negotiations.

Haggling is not true negotiation because values are not being created. Instead, the existing value is being split into smaller pieces, and when value is split it leaves less for each party to take. A zero-sum negotiation is haggling, while a collaborative negotiation is bargaining.

So, what could the father have taught his son in the chocolate chip scenario?

Son: Could I have some chocolate chips, please?

Father: Maybe so, but why do you want chips?

Son: Because I'm hungry.

Father: Okay. But why chocolate chips, rather than an apple or a cookie?

Son: Because chocolate chips are yummy.

Father: I agree! They're tasty, all right, but they aren't very healthy. I'd prefer to see you eat something a little more nutritious, to help you grow big and strong. And if you're hungry, I wonder if chips will really fill you up enough.

Son: You're right—they wouldn't fill me up unless I ate a lot of them. So can I have them all?

Father: So, you want to satisfy your hunger and eat something tasty. That makes sense. And I want you to satisfy your hunger too, but with something healthier. What if you were to eat an apple to fill you up, and then you could have 10 chocolate chips as a treat?

Son: Hmmm. OK, Dad. I'll eat the apple and then have 10 chocolate chips.

Admittedly I probably oversimplified this example, especially when you consider kids and chocolate chips. And I'm sure it wouldn't go down quite that easily with my own kids. But the purpose of the example is to show how the number of negotiated variables can be expanded, and how a negotiation's focus can be shifted from zero-sum to collaboration.

ESSENTIAL TAKEAWAYS

- Take your time to gain a thorough understanding of all the variables involved in the negotiation before making any decisions.

- Pay attention to all signals your counterpart gives you.

- Make sure you get something in return for any concessions you make, and avoid making unilateral concessions, especially under pressure.

- Haggling means splitting existing value into smaller pieces. Bargaining means adding on value to be split. Always bargain instead of haggle.

The Phases of Negotiation: Postnegotiation

PHASE 7: CLOSING THE DEAL

It's time for you to close the contract when you feel (or know) you've presented the other party with a package that meets their needs, while still achieving as close to your goals as possible. You only reach this phase when you can answer yes to these questions:

- Is everyone on board with the demands? Have you locked them in?

- Does the other party have authority to make a decision? Are all the people required to make a decision present?

- Has your counterpart conducted negotiations with your competitors or other opposing negotiating parties? (Without this step, they might not have the information needed to make a decision.)

- Are they working under a deadline? (Many negotiations conclude before the deadline because decisions are accelerated by time pressure rather than complete agreement between parties.)

There are many ways to close a negotiation, some better than others. The ideal way is by reaching an agreement organically, after you've gone back and forth in the bargaining phase. But sometimes agreements are reached in negative ways and should be avoided, if possible. The following methods are attempts to close a deal in mostly a negative way, often leaving the counterpart feeling pushed into an agreement.

Make a Threat

A negotiation should always end in summarizing the demands put forth. Once you have the other party's demands, you could test boundaries by only partially meeting the demands. This method involves promoting only the demands you agree with and ignoring the rest:

> We're not able to go above the offer we are presenting now, which meets most of your requirements. We think that is a good compromise. Keep in mind that we might not be able to guarantee our terms/prices if you delay in your decision, since the market is ever changing.

You are essentially threatening to walk away from the deal if the other party can't meet your proposal. There is a risk, of course, in going this route. If the other party trusts you (as we discussed in Phase 3 with interpersonal relationship building), they will take you at your word that you can't compromise more. However, they can also decide you're bluffing or lying to get a better deal.

If you're unable to reach a conclusion, you can essentially just say, "Take it or leave it." This threatens the other party to either come to your agreement or risk you walking away from a potential deal. Making a convincing argument for this move requires knowing when to draw the line, since it could end up costly if they don't believe you.

Propose a New Agreement

In the event you're unable to secure the other party's commitment, or if new demands arise, take a break to consider new alternatives. You might need to reevaluate your goals for the negotiation (but if making any concessions be sure they are not more than you're willing to make). Perhaps presenting your package differently might appeal more to the other party. For example, promising delivery time improvements may serve you better than a price reduction.

Make a Small Unilateral Concession

It might be worth making a unilateral concession if you believe the disagreement between you is minimal. The offer must have a limited value, and the other party must be bound by a promise. Let's say you're negotiating with your spouse about where to go on your next vacation. Your spouse wants to go to an all-inclusive resort but you don't. You could make a unilateral concession by accepting an all-inclusive resort if you have dinner outside the resort one evening.

Retract the Offer

When you can't come to a reasonable agreement, you might retract an offer made during the bargaining phase. This is definitely a last resort approach, and never threaten to rescind an offer unless you don't have alternate options. Negotiators using this tactic may subtly raise or change their demands when summarizing negotiation terms. Imagine your daughter asks for her allowance to be increased to $10 a week. You discuss chores she must do in order to attain this, like taking out the trash, doing the dishes, and cleaning up her room. She agrees, and when she summarizes the agreement between you, she subtly says her allowance is increased to $11 a week. She retracted the original offer of $10 to make it $11 instead.

PHASE 8: SIGNING THE DEAL

Once a contract has been reached, all that remains is to sign the agreement. This is the last step in the negotiation process. Celebrate your victory after it has been won, not before! Keep in mind that previous verbal agreements are not binding. Verbal agreements can't be enforced if they are not directly accepted, and if they haven't been given a definite period in which to consider them. A legal contract or other form of official confirmation of the deal you've negotiated must be created. Ensuring that all agreements are in writing will prevent many future conflicts and problems.

What kind of conflicts can arise without a binding contract? The other party may claim to have misunderstood the deal. Or they could make a last-minute bluff to sweeten a deal they weren't entirely happy with in the end. Or you could interpret the terms of the deal differently than your counterpart does. Perhaps, at the last minute, the other party simply changes their mind when you meet to sign the agreement. You had a verbal agreement that they no longer will abide by. If you celebrated early by getting production going, placing orders, or spending money you thought was coming in but isn't anymore, you've put yourself in a weak position to counterargue.

Let's say you reach an agreement with a buyer after rounds and rounds of hard negotiations. It is decided that the buyer will draft a contract of the agreement you've reached. Then the day you expect the contract in your inbox, you get the following message:

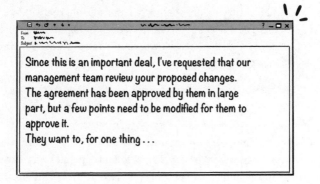

Since this is an important deal, I've requested that our management team review your proposed changes.
The agreement has been approved by them in large part, but a few points need to be modified for them to approve it.
They want to, for one thing . . .

A very unexpected and unpleasant surprise! There are a few options available to you:

- Grant the additional concessions. Hopefully, you have enough negotiating room in your budget, or the customer is willing to shoulder these costs.

- Stand your ground and say no, and risk losing not only money, but time and resources.

- As far as the modifications required by the client goes, you are entitled to compensation. Even oral agreements are legally binding, but obviously very hard to document and prove. It is possible that the buyer claims you misunderstood him. Your proposal was only a draft, he claims. Proof is a heavy burden to bear.

- Stall. Consider the new demands over a longer period of time and determine whether the customer has any alternatives, or whether you conceding is imperative to them. Then you can make a new offer and continue negotiating once you understand your negotiating position and alternatives. Treat it like a new negotiation with new terms. Keep your cool in the face of the customer's tactical gambit. Consider it instead as a signal for purchasing.

The best way to avoid having to choose any of these options is to conclude every negotiation with a summary of the agreements or outcomes reached—*then put this in writing*. I can't stress the importance of this phase enough! It's even more important to put things in writing and review them when the formal agreement is drafted by a party not present at the negotiation, or in some cases where the negotiations are conducted in another language (via a translator). To avoid these issues, make notes throughout the negotiations. In essence, before you move to a new segment, always summarize what was discussed regarding the current parameter. By asking your counterpart to summarize, you gain a better understanding of where that party stands, and therefore build a binding contract that you both can agree on.

PHASE 9: POSTMORTEM

Congratulations! You've successfully navigated a negotiation by preparing, built trust with your negotiating counterpart by creating interpersonal relationships, argued your demands and listened to the other party's counterarguments, bargained for a deal, reached a conclusion you're both happy with, and put it all down in writing. Now that the deal is underway, it's time for your postmortem. In this phase, we examine the results of a negotiation and evaluate whether we can continue negotiations in the future. You can also use a checklist to organize your thoughts and evaluate how a negotiation went on paper.

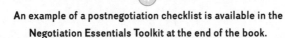

An example of a postnegotiation checklist is available in the Negotiation Essentials Toolkit at the end of the book.

Negotiation and transaction outcomes have much more to do with personal relationships than with price, quantity, or other factors. Our emotions play a large role in negotiations, and an agreement can't work as planned if one party feels like a loser. It is only possible to implement and enforce an agreement if both parties are satisfied with it.

It is imperative your counterparts can present any agreement to their organizations with a financial result that can be justified. In the long run, there must be enough short-term and long-term gains to make the agreement interesting, not just an equal division of profits, costs, and risks. Obviously, the deal should also be better than the alternative options available. Help the other party prepare their internal arguments for when they present the agreement in-house.

Both parties have to be satisfied with the outcome.

There shouldn't be any feelings of cheating, insecurity, or manipulation caused by clever tactical maneuvers. Both parties should feel happy with how they managed the negotiation, in addition to the outcome. It is important no one feels they've lost face during negotiations; otherwise, expect negative consequences down the line. For starters, all the interpersonal relationship-building you did during the opening phase could dissolve if the other party feels taken advantage of. They could also hesitate to negotiate again later, retaliate by not renewing the contract or raising prices in the future, or even bad-mouth you to other prospective negotiators. Many agreements throughout history have resulted in winners and losers. After all, the Treaty of Versailles ended WWI—but also laid the foundation for WWII.

To avoid dire situations, you should have already utilized the opening phase to establish communication channels and extend personal relationships. But you also should maintain those communication channels beyond the negotiation table. People don't like partners who show consideration only on the day the agreement is written or when it's being renewed. When consideration is received only when we prove useful to others, we feel taken advantage of. Ensure that everyone affected by the agreement, but not present at the negotiations, is kept informed of the agreement's content and objectives.

PHASE 10: DECIDING WHETHER TO CONTINUE THE RELATIONSHIP

Ideally, both parties have kept to the deal reached during the negotiation and put in writing. If the need still exists, and the personal relations are good, it is likely an agreement will be renewed. However, you may have to rework parts of the agreement and possibly deal with a number of external factors and modifications. Some things might have changed since you first reached a deal and drafted a contract:

- New individuals have been appointed to key positions. Their experiences and contacts could differ, along with their views about how the negotiating party's original needs should be met. Relationships between individuals are the backbone of business.

- New technical solutions can change how a deal is carried out, or the very need for the deal.

- There may be a change in the economic, political, or social environment.

- New budgets may restrict or potentially expand the current deal.

The decision to renew or discontinue an agreement is not always an easy process. If only one party wishes to withdraw from the agreement, the divorce can be painful and difficult. It could strain professional relationships or cause the other party to pursue unilateral solutions, which only serve their interests. The risk of losing a business relationship is a definite possibility when ending an agreed deal.

Let's look at an example of how not continuing a deal can be detrimental to both parties: A boutique hotel owner hires an interior designer to develop plans for redesigning guest rooms. They have a great partnership, and the owner and designer agree to continue working together on future hotels that the owner is hoping to expand to in the next few years. The designer is committed to a multiyear contract—after all, she has a great relationship with the owner, who supports her design vision. And the pay isn't too shabby either! A year into their contract, the hotel owner unexpectedly sells the hotel to a large chain of hotels, and there's no longer a need for the designer because the chain designs all their hotels to look similar.

The designer never thought to add a clause to her contract about what would happen to her job if the hotel owner sells his hotel, and this move comes as a blow to her. The owner didn't even warn her he was planning this. Not only is she out of a job, but she no longer trusts the hotel owner to be open and communicative in the future, souring any future potential partnership.

This is a common mistake made when negotiating a long-term agreement: not including divorce settlements in the agreement. Divorce settlements should be governed by set guidelines from the beginning, and conditions that take the parties' wishes into account are more likely to be agreed upon during a period of good personal relations rather than after the divorce is final. The postmortem of this negotiation deal shows how important it is to plan ahead!

It's impossible to predict the future after signing an agreement; there are plenty of blind alleys to navigate ahead. But conducting a postmortem of your negotiations will certainly help you travel those unknown alleys. Doing this, along with all the phases discussed, will help you be the most insightful and successful negotiator you can be.

ESSENTIAL TAKEAWAYS

- To close a negotiation, ensure that all demands and needs have been met by summarizing the outcome.

- A successful agreement should make both parties feel good about themselves and the deal reached.

- The decision to renew a deal comes from factors you find in your postmortem of the deal.

- Learn from your mistakes after a deal is implemented to avoid making them again in future negotiations.

The Five Styles of Negotiation

Imagine you are sitting in a negotiation with a client. The negotiation has gone smoothly so far—you've both been calm, respectful, and constructive in negotiating the details. Each of you has presented offers and counteroffers, and it seems like you're ready to land on a deal when the client suddenly says: "You know, now that I've thought about it further, your price is way too high!"

Many negotiations go this way. All seems well until one party throws out an unexpected wrench—in this case, pushing back on price even though you both seemed to have been on the same page. You try to determine your client's needs before responding to her concern about the price. That conversation goes something like this:

>**You:** In comparison with what is our offer more expensive?

>**Client:** Your competitors.

>**You:** Why do you think we are too expensive? Could you elaborate on how your other offers compare?

Client: There's no way we'll be able to work together unless you lower your price.

You: I would appreciate it if you could specify what you think is incorrectly priced, and what you think the correct price should be.

Client: This is pointless, you clearly don't understand market conditions and competition. Ideally, we would like an offer with better terms and prices tomorrow. We're done for today.

What would be an appropriate way for a professional negotiator to handle a situation like the one just described? Should they give in, counterargue, or simply leave the meeting?

Every person negotiates differently. There are differences in how each person perceives negotiation as well as differences in how each person reacts to stress and pressure during a negotiation. It is essential to know your counterpart's negotiation style before adjusting your response. Additionally, it is crucial to understand your own negotiation style. Do you consider yourself to be combative? What can lead to this behavior? Do you blame your opponent's behavior? Do you blame your manager? What even *are* the other styles of negotiation available to you?

Identifying the various types of behaviors and negotiation styles, and knowing which tools to use to deal with them, are important skills for all negotiators. The following are the five types of negotiation styles I've identified: combative, collaborative, concessional, compromising, and stalling. All negotiations can fall under one, or a combination, of these styles. Let's look at each.

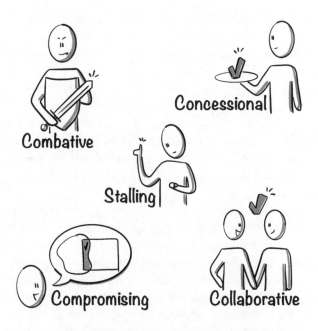

THE COMBATIVE NEGOTIATOR

It is important for negotiators to recognize that the behavior displayed by the client in the example earlier in this chapter is combative, which means she uses aggressive tactics to gain the upper hand. As such, it is crucial for negotiators to be equipped with the necessary skills to defuse such situations, as well as other surprising scenarios that may arise during negotiations. Despite her demands for a lower price, she refuses to talk about her concerns to find middle ground. Since she's giving no information and adding a time constraint ("We would like a better offer tomorrow"), she's creating pressure, in turn making you feel insecure about what you bring to the table. The client reacted aggressively, so any relationship-building that existed at the beginning of the negotiation is likely gone.

You might not handle the situation properly if you do not take the right steps. There are two alternatives negotiators often only see in situations like this: ending the negotiation by lowering the price or getting angry and shutting down further discussion. But there are other effective methods available. Take a second to think about why the other party might use combative tactics.

A combative negotiator wants to create a sense of insecurity and inferiority in the opposing party because a stressed negotiator is more likely to give up and flee. Negotiators may also be combative because they went into a negotiation without a clear strategy, or their own communication style is a mystery to them. They tend to avoid opening up in the first place due to fear, insecurity, and being underprepared. This leads to the combative negotiator resorting to bluffing, ultimatums, pressuring, remaining silent, or belittling their counterpart to hide their own insecurities or force a concession.

Other factors that could influence combativeness are internal business factors, like a bad economy or declining profits. When a company faces outside pressure, so do its employees. An employee negotiating on behalf of a company may resort to combativeness to generate faster or bigger profits, essentially also creating job security for themselves.

Whatever the reasons, a combative negotiator will, by nature, have one goal: to compel you to make unilateral concessions so they can win. In this situation, you as the noncombative negotiator are the one who bears all the costs of any gains made.

How to Deal with Combative Negotiators

Dealing with combative negotiators can be emotional work, depending on your personality and how you tend to respond to aggression: flight or fight. Don't let your emotions lead you to make rash emotional decisions in a negotiation. A trap is just around the corner if you don't watch out.

If you're feeling overwhelmed by a combative negotiator, you may need to take a break. There are many tactics to defuse the situation, but before you can choose the right one you'll need to consider these questions: Is the other party intentionally acting defensively, or is it only a subconscious reaction? Do you think the other party is using the wrong words or speaking in an inappropriate tone? Does the harshness of that person's demands frighten you? To communicate clearly, there must be a clear distinction between combat and clear-cut communication.

Consider the following tactics to respond to a combative negotiation.

Silence

Sit in silence in response to an aggressive comment or question, and keep your cool if someone provokes you. Avoid engaging in an argument with the other party, and let them finish their point (even if it's wrong) instead of immediately jumping on the defensive. Maintain your composure and your professionalism, and you may save the negotiation from breaking down. Silence can be uncomfortable, but learn to embrace it as a tool to regroup—even if it's just in your mind.

Take a Break to Regroup

There is no guarantee that keeping silent will end in a positive result. If it doesn't, you can always stall the negotiation. Tell the other party you don't feel the negotiation is worthwhile at this time and arrange a new meeting. Be mild in manner, but firm in your message.

Redirect

Communicate clearly and openly how this aggressive style won't work for you in this negotiation. You should demonstrate how you can achieve a better outcome for both of you in lieu of combat by saying:

> This negotiation is going in an unwelcome direction, and if we continue like this we won't get anywhere. Let's instead examine how we can collaborate in order for you to become more successful, but not at my expense.

Make a Concession

Take the other party's side by making a concession. To achieve this, there needs to be a lot of room for negotiation, and it won't work if you get caught off guard by the combative nature of the meeting. You've probably heard the phrase "it's not about winning the battle but the war." This is what we're aiming for. Giving the counterpart something of value to them perhaps doesn't really cost you anything. If your spouse asks you to empty the dishwasher, it may not be worth it to negotiate yourself out of it. Just accept the chore, and you both benefit (your spouse because the dishes are done, and you because there will be clean dishes next time you need one).

Ask Questions

Sometimes it's necessary to ask questions to test the other party and enable that party to appreciate the potential dangers of continuing the conflict. Your chances of defusing the situation and winning that person's trust are better if you can establish two-way communication. Do this by asking the other party to repeat any arguments and concerns. Keep that person talking as much as possible to get to the root of the problem. The more that person feels free to express concerns, the more open he or she will be to finding a solution.

Change Negotiators

If you can't build an interpersonal connection, or see eye to eye with the combative negotiator, it may be time to bring in a new negotiator. Sometimes the cause of the combative behavior is the person more than the content of the negotiation. I am certain you have tried to meet an individual whom you never met before, only to not particularly like that individual. Perhaps you don't even know why you dislike that person. The same thing can happen in a negotiation. Don't let bad personal chemistry destroy the agreement. Be mature enough to realize that you may be the root of the problem and step aside. I often ask managers how they react if an employee asks to be replaced in a negotiation. Managers who start criticizing such employees and dismissing their concerns may be very wrong.

Simply Fight Back

If you have a strong position, like having a monopoly, being the only supplier that is able to deliver, or perhaps just being the most competitive negotiator and willing to pay the price for defeating the other party, you should respond to combat with combat. The only time this is recommended is if you don't want any involvement with the other party in the future and have exhausted all other options. Fighting back will lead to negative results, including loss of collaboration, interpersonal relationships, and trust; potential retaliation by the opposing party in future negotiations; and the loss of the goal in the negotiation itself (whether it was a promotion, making a sale, getting a discount, or anything else you would negotiate).

Assertiveness Is Not the Same as Combativeness

Don't confuse a tough and uncompromising attitude with combativeness. A combative negotiation style is characterized by condescending behavior, provocative language, dishonesty, and exploitation for one's own gain. Negotiators who are clear-cut and strong on their negotiation points, and who try to be open and motivating in their approach, are not combative.

Communication is a two-way street. When one party is combative and uncommunicative, there isn't a way forward. Likewise, if both parties are combative, negotiations get deadlocked. That's why creating good personal relationships with people and generating constructive dialogue is important to the goal of everyone involved in a negotiation.

THE COLLABORATIVE NEGOTIATOR

Collaboration is based on the highest level of trust. It requires open and honest communication between the parties that is driven by a willingness to listen and understand other parties' needs and requirements. Collaboration does not mean shirking the issues or relinquishing your own needs or position of power. The purpose of collaboration is to make the stake as large as possible for the benefit of both parties.

An example of a collaborative negotiation is when one side of the negotiation actively supports the counterpart in reducing costs, liabilities, risk, and time. For example, two truck companies are working together on a delivery contract and discover that company A can run their trucks at a 15 percent lower cost than company B. The two parties then agree that company A will run all the deliveries using their trucks, while company B will compensate company A for delivery costs and split the difference on what they saved.

Collaborative negotiators take an open and honest approach to listening, asking, and answering questions. They don't play games to try to catch you by surprise, unlike combative negotiators. To collaborative negotiators, the other party is an equal partner in the meeting. When conflict happens, they try to develop alternative solutions based on a comprehensive analysis of needs, problems, and opportunities on the table.

The two parties may not necessarily benefit equally from collaboration. It is essential that your proposal is better than every other alternative available to the other party in order for it to be successful. For an agreement to be successful, both parties must be treated equally, accurate information must be provided, and the reasons for the agreement must be explained openly.

The Negative Side of Collaboration

While collaboration may sound like the ideal style for all negotiations, it's not all rosy. Attempting to cooperate at the negotiation table can lead to a host of problems you may not immediately think about.

If you are a collaborative negotiator, your openness may be perceived as a sign of weakness or inexperience. An opposing negotiator may try to take advantage of this misconceived weakness, possibly combatively. When you are open and sharing cost and values, the counterpart could abuse that openness by not responding in kind. I recommend collaboration, sharing, and openness, but never at the expense of naivety. If you're not careful with how open you are in a negotiation, you risk giving too much away. And by doing so, you easily become naive. If you agree with the counterpart to share your data and the counterpart isn't sharing their numbers, the counterpart is able to see the true size of the pizza and you aren't. That means they can slice the pizza as they like.

Another caution about collaborative negotiation is it requires trust, and it takes time and effort to build that kind of interpersonal chemistry. It's not always possible before negotiations start, so you might not have that solid foundation in place before you can collaborate.

Collaboration doesn't always work in all negotiations. When the other party prioritizes short-term gains, for example, they won't be keeping collaboration in mind. They will likely instead choose a combative style with threats, confrontations, and pressure games to meet their end goal, instead of thinking how it will affect their goal in the long term.

How to Use the Collaboration Style

There is no one-size-fits-all solution to collaboration. Collaborating demands serious commitments from you and the other party. And parts of the collaborative style are already built into a negotiation process from the beginning. For example, a cooperative mindset is essential for opening and analyzing negotiations. To accomplish this, you must display generosity, be open to constructive ideas, and avoid allowing your emotions to dictate your actions. When feelings of insecurity, fighting, and deadlock arise during a negotiation, asking for a break is the best way to handle them.

In order to figure out where to collaborate, consider variables in the negotiation that you can compromise on or collaborate on. With your negotiation planner (see Chapter 6), map out your variables and take a moment to consider whether they offer much room for negotiation. Do you have the option of giving more or taking less? What are the consequences if you do give or take on those variables? Remember, collaboration is all about equal parts give and take, so mapping out where you have flexibility ahead of time helps build a framework for collaboration.

Whenever you're seeking information from another party, it is imperative you also open yourself up to them. Openness leads to a culture of trust. Embrace the opportunity to open up sooner rather than later. However, take care to not reveal too much too soon. At the very least you should express interest, options, and directions: "Our team will investigate ways to reduce delivery time. The process could be shortened. It might require a little extra effort, but I think it will still be worthwhile."

In this example, you're opening up all options to your counterpart, but taking care to keep specifics to yourself until you learn more about their expectations.

This negotiation style is for you if you want to establish a long-term negotiation relationship with your counterpart, to find the best deal that works for both parties, when good interpersonal chemistry already exists or was established, and to avoid conflict. However, be wary of how collaboration can backfire. It may make you seem like a weaker negotiator to some combative-focused negotiators. And you must take care to not give away too much or you'll lose in the end.

THE CONCESSIONAL NEGOTIATOR

The concession-oriented negotiator is one who gives something away without getting anything back. In general, if you are forced to pick between concession or combative behavior, please choose combat. Not that I endorse combative behavior, but comparing it to concession, combative negotiators generate better results. (However, if I really had to choose a style, I would always choose collaboration.)

For example, a company is looking for a supplier. The company says, "I apologize, but we cannot use you as a supplier. Your prices are too high." The supplier responds, "Well, I can't do much regarding prices." This conversation continues:

Company: How much can you do?

Supplier: I can offer you a 3 percent discount.

Company: Unfortunately, I don't think that's enough

Supplier: Well, 5 percent is the maximum I'm authorized to give.

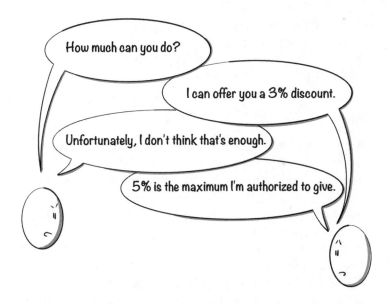

The supplier appears to be trying to escape an unpleasant negotiation by making too many concessions, which is perhaps the most dangerous course of action. If you make too many concessions without ensuring you're getting something in return, you stand to lose too much. Negotiators tend to make too many concessions when they're stressed, feeling insecure, or under pressure. Smart negotiators can easily take advantage of that. If you ever feel stressed or pressured in a negotiation, take a break. It's as simple as saying, "I'd like to stretch my legs a little." In addition to relaxing, the break can allow you to let go of insecurity, which often leads you to consider alternatives to unilateral concessions.

Concession-oriented negotiators also tend to never really learn how to handle conflict, a skill essential to negotiation. It is critical to open up communication and question what the other party demands, which can be uncomfortable for some negotiators. Choosing to stick to this style inevitably leads to negotiations that end rather quickly with no benefit to the conceding party.

Concede Tactically, Not Entirely

Sometimes, a concession is a tactical move. If you establish how much negotiation room you have on your variables in advance, you can generate "negotiating currency." In the negotiation, you will trade this currency for a variety of benefits. The concession is like making a deposit in your very own "goodwill account." You and your counterpart both acknowledge that you gave up something for free. And the other party is more likely to do business with you if he succeeds early in the negotiation. This can cause his guard to lower and anticipate a simple solution moving forward. The strategy you employ by showing goodwill leads him to invest time, resources, and personal prestige into the negotiation. If you raise your demands later, he might not be able to break off the negotiations after putting in so much time. The objective is to not sacrifice profits or personal needs, nor to take unplanned risks. Instead, make trades in the form of money, time, warranties, extras, and so on.

Even when a negotiation is deadlocked, don't make unilateral concessions without obtaining something in return. Choose a concession that you know you can get something back on (e.g., if I give you x and I can expect y, we can move forward with z) and show great firmness in explaining why you are making the concession. This could allow your counterpart to open up and continue the negotiation. This is the only point on which you are giving in. Whenever you are squeezed by someone without giving anything back, avoid responding by making another concession.

THE COMPROMISING NEGOTIATOR

The compromising negotiator is one who meets their counterpart's demands halfway. This involves reaching a solution geometrically in the middle of an original demand and a new (undesirable) demand. A negotiator might take a pragmatic approach and use this strategy to get out of a combative negotiation. Compromising allows a negotiator to get as close as possible to their goal when the other party refuses to budge any further. As a result, a compromising negotiator might have to lose more than they wanted to reach a compromise. This is why this strategy is a negative one: a compromising negotiator often haggles to meet in the middle, which means losing more than if you were to collaborate to find value for both parties.

Consider this example of a buyer and seller negotiating payment terms:

> **Buyer:** We can't proceed until we clarify one point in your quote. It appears that you have only offered us a term of payment of 30 days, rather than the 90 days we requested.

> **Seller:** We can only offer a maximum of 30 days.

> **Buyer:** I can't accept the quote if that is the case. I can't compromise on our 90-day requirement.

> **Seller:** Well, our usual terms are 10, 20, and 30 days. It has already been my pleasure to offer you the best credit.

Buyer: Then I can't accept your offer.

Seller: For your convenience, I can extend you to 45 days. This is my best and last offer—we've never offered as much to a customer!

Buyer: You offered us 30 days, but I requested 90. When you move your offer to 45, you're only giving 15 days more, but the jump from 90 to 45 is much bigger!

Seller: OK, how about 60 days? Are you willing to accept that?

First, both parties need to state their case in order to reach a compromise. They continue to argue despite the fact that neither is listening to the other. It is common for their statements to be biased and untrue.

Threats are usually used to force the other party to concede or to see if the threat is genuine if neither party wants to give in. They usually arrive at a solution somewhere between the original and new positions, in the geometrical middle. Each party does not wish to lose out on the division and give or obtain more than their counterpart.

Untruthful arguments cause us to lose trust in negotiators. In this example, the seller initially only offers 10-, 20-, or 30-day payments, yet offers the buyer 45- and 60-day payments when pushed. It takes only 15 seconds for the seller to deliver the best offer ever made. Although 90 days was not negotiable, the buyer ended up accepting 60 days.

The other party is coerced into abandoning a position by orchestrating facts, faking it, bluffing, applying time pressure, promising future compensation, and direct threats: "If you don't accommodate us, we will . . ." The negotiation process requires a great deal of effort on the part of the negotiation team. Rather than asking and answering questions, they prefer to argue.

A compromising negotiator and a conceding negotiator differ in their approaches to the negotiation process. Compromising negotiators seek to find a middle ground or a win-win solution that benefits both parties. They are willing to negotiate on various aspects of the deal in order to reach an agreement that is acceptable to both sides.

On the other hand, conceding negotiators give in to the demands of the other party in order to reach an agreement quickly. They are often focused on the short-term outcome of the negotiation and may prioritize speed over the long-term implications of the deal. A conceding negotiator may be willing to sacrifice their own interests to reach an agreement, which may lead to an unfavorable outcome for them in the long run.

How to Deal with the Compromising Negotiator

It's impossible to negotiate constructively if the other party won't tell you the background of his or her requirements. As a result, you're facing a compromise negotiation that looks more like combat. The method you choose in those cases is often the same as in combat.

By offering alternatives, a better method can be achieved. Whenever possible, accommodate your counterpart, but always demand something in return. A genuine compromise can only be found in this manner. In your manner, be mild, but in your substance, be firm.

Trying to say yes, but demanding something in return you know the other party cannot give you, may help you overcome the other party's demands.

THE STALLING NEGOTIATOR

You're at the end of a negotiation after several days of back-and-forth answering questions and concerns. There is a whiteboard in the room with a summary of your pricing your counterpart has negotiated on the services you offer. However, even though it's a number you both reached together, the client asks, "Is this your best offer?" You're surprised the question is asked as you think you've met all of the client's expectations and requirements. When you reply that it is your best offer, the client says, "Well, then I'll call you in two weeks to let you know if you got the order!" The statement catches you off guard and you walk away insecure and uncertain, thinking, *Did I just waste my time on this negotiation? Is my competition offering a better quote? Should I contact her and make a better offer, or wait for her response?*

Stalling involves delaying the conclusion of the negotiation or the resolution of certain issues, often to strengthen one's own position. A negotiator who stalls creates pressure for the other party to reach a better agreement by leaving them uncertain. As we've learned, an insecure negotiator is more likely to make mistakes or unilateral concessions. A stalling negotiator takes advantage of this by putting off a decision in the hopes that the other party will reach out in their eagerness to close the deal. A negotiator may also stall in order to gain more knowledge. That party may reach out to competitors for other offers or wait for input from their boss. They may even realize they didn't prepare enough before the negotiation and use the stall to conduct more research.

Negotiators may also use this tactic because they are insecure or inexperienced. When faced with an unsatisfactory agreement or conflict, they wish to put it off until later. It's important to note that stalling doesn't always improve a negotiator's position, but it can act as an escape mechanism that may prove more useful than a concession that's unplanned.

How to Deal with a Stalling Negotiator

Stalling negotiators run the risk of having negotiations end entirely if the other party believes they are uncooperative or unprofessional. Additionally, negotiators who delay in making a decision risk having another party get the deal. Your negotiating counterpart might take advantage of your stalling as well by making their offer to another negotiator. For example, a manager who stalls when their employee asks for a raise runs the risk of the employee taking their talent to another company who can offer what they want.

What should you do when facing a negotiator who stalls for time? Always get a binding option or agreement in writing from the stalling party. During a negotiation, confirm everything in writing and use the phrase "if I don't hear anything back, I assume we are in agreement about . . ." Use the summary of your agreement to confirm what the stalling negotiator may not say in words.

If it's in your best interests, you could also wait out the stalling negotiator. Striking is an example of this. When a teachers union strikes, the teachers generate pressure on the school district administrators by staying out of classrooms, which means students are home instead of at school. This in turn angers and frustrates parents. All this mounting pressure is intended to motivate administrators to come to the table quicker and meet the union's demands.

You can also consider your alternatives when negotiating with someone who stalls. Negotiate with all available alternatives—other parties, suppliers, or customers. Any alternative to the counterpart who is stalling is better than wasting time. It may also be necessary to find other parties to negotiate with if the current negotiation threatens your interests.

TEN ORANGES, FIVE STYLES

Let's see the five styles we've just discussed in action. Two teams are competing for all 10 oranges in a bowl. How does each team try to get as close to 10 oranges as possible?

Combative Negotiators

The teams resort to combative behavior to try to get all 10 oranges for themselves. They fight over the oranges by threatening each other with harsh words. Eventually, harsh words turn into physical threats. They punch, claw, and scramble to get to the bowl and claim all oranges first. Neither team ends up winning cleanly; physical and verbal combat leaves them all battered and bruised both physically and mentally. Even if one team does manage to snatch all 10 oranges, the way they got to them leaves a bitter taste in everyone's mouth.

Concessional Negotiators

In this style, the negotiators avoid conflict by leaving all the oranges to the other party. Effectively, one party gives up without a fight. And if both parties give up, it turns into an endless loop of: "You take them, I'm sure you'll have better use for them." "No, you take them, I'm sure you need them more!" "No, we insist, you should take them!"

Stalling Negotiators

The teams want to find a solution on who should take the oranges, so they stall for time to figure out how. Stalling teams may leave the room to go have coffee with their group—perhaps the problem will solve itself. Or team members could use the time to come up with a new strategy for getting all or some oranges. Maybe the other team's resolve will waver while they wait and they will cave or come up with a solution. But while the teams stall, the main conflict remains: Who will take the oranges? No one wins while there is a standstill.

Compromising Negotiators

The teams decide to compromise and divide the 10 oranges, but each team wants more oranges than the other team. Each team will try to use compromising as a tool over the other: "We'll agree to split the oranges, but we should get 7 and we'll let you walk away with 3." "Why should you walk away with more? If we get six, we'll let you have four, which is more than you're offering us!" The offer of a compromise does not lead to any solution acceptable to both teams. Both want all 10 oranges, but if they have to compromise, neither of them wants to look like a loser.

Collaborative Negotiators

Both teams cooperate to try to solve how many oranges each should get. Before they can do so, however, they need more information. When are the oranges to be used, and what are they going to be used for? The teams discuss openly and find out that team A will juice the oranges and team B will make marmalade, and both teams will use the oranges immediately for their next breakfast. Now, they are able to find multiple solutions:

1. They could split the oranges equally and still have enough juice and marmalade for breakfast.

2. They research recipes and find that marmalade requires more oranges than juicing does, so they split them 60/40.

3. Team A relinquishes more oranges to team B, with the understanding that team B will provide team A with marmalade when the batch is ready (or invite them to breakfast to enjoy some marmalade).

By honestly disclosing their intentions to each other, the parties established that their needs were not contradictory and that both parties could have their needs met. This way, both parties feel like winners.

PICKING THE RIGHT NEGOTIATION STYLE

Unfortunately, the world isn't black or white! Preparing for a negotiation would be a lot easier if we knew what we were getting ahead of time, and if the other negotiator would stick to it the whole time.

A combative negotiator would be easier to deal with if he or she always behaved combatively, while a conceding negotiator acts concession-oriented consistently. The collaborative negotiator can turn combative at times, while the compromising negotiator can become concessional. You cannot be sure how the counterpart is going to react because you do not always know their needs, their subconscious drives, or the feelings that govern their decision-making ahead of a negotiation. As a result of so much uncertainty, you can't plan your entire negotiation strategy in advance or structure it around any single approach or style choice. Some negotiators select a single negotiation method and stick with it throughout the entire negotiation. Other negotiators are inflexible and try to match the negotiation to how they imagined it would go, rather than shifting their strategy or their style choice to reflect the dynamic actually on the table.

The professional negotiator must be responsive and adaptable, willing to go with the flow and adjust styles as the negotiation unfolds. Whenever you find the negotiation is slipping from your grip—take a break! Analyze what is happening and decide if you need to switch your style or make use of a different tactic to get the negotiation back on track and moving in the direction you want it to go.

ESSENTIAL TAKEAWAYS

- It's important to be flexible. You may need to change your style if it isn't moving the negotiation forward. Know your counterpart's negotiation style before adjusting your response.

- Remember, every person has a different negotiation style. Some may choose to switch it up—the style they start with may not be their style at the end.

- Use breaks in a negotiation to reassess or readjust your negotiation style, if necessary.

- Don't be afraid of combative behavior. You can use compromise to get out of a combative negotiation.

- Combining cooperation and collaboration is one of the best ways to achieve your goals in a negotiation.

PART III

BEYOND
THE
ESSENTIALS

CHAPTER

10

The Principles of NegoEconomics

Now that you've learned all the basics of negotiation, let's delve deeper into how NegoEconomics and SMARTnership help you succeed in any negotiation. As already discussed, NegoEconomics is the asymmetric value between the parties' costs and values. A SMARTnership is a partnership characterized by a high level of trust, transparency, and communication between the parties involved. Both parties are committed to creating long-term value and working together to achieve mutual goals, rather than simply maximizing short-term gains for themselves.

SMARTnership and NegoEconomics are award-winning negotiation and relationship strategies implemented successfully in hundreds of organizations worldwide—among others, the Canadian government, Novo Nordisk, Rolls-Royce, Samsung, Vestas, ThermoFisher, and LEGO.

Many people perceive the wiggle room in any negotiation as the difference between the highest price a buyer is willing to pay and the lowest price a seller can come down to. In this scenario, it's only possible to strike a deal if the buyer can pay a price above the seller's threshold of pain. The real room for negotiation becomes much larger if you learn how to create NegoEconomics. I can only emphasize the importance of continuous learning and improvement in a SMARTnership with both parties regularly exchanging knowledge, ideas, and feedback to enhance the partnership and drive innovation.

FINDING NegoEconomics IN A NEGOTIATION

Our studies indicate that approximately 40 percent of the actual room for negotiation is never exploited because negotiators have not learned to identify and utilize the potential of NegoEconomics.[1] You can locate the NegoEconomics by finding the answers to these questions:

- What can I do to assist the other party to reduce their costs and risks or to increase their profits?

- What can the other party do to assist me in reducing my costs and risks or to increase my profits?

- What would a partnership look like if we have the common goal of reducing costs and risks on both sides?

Regardless of whether you negotiate with your spouse, your child, yourself, your manager, your employees, or your bank, insurance company, or tax authorities, there is value hidden in the transaction that is rarely, if ever, identified. In the past 25 years, I've looked at thousands of companies and found that some are more successful than others. I researched and studied the way they negotiate deals to see how big or small the share of their success (or lack thereof) was attributable to their skills and understanding of negotiation. I found that the companies that were doing better in collaborative situations, whether it was buying, selling, managing projects, or otherwise, succeed because of their mastery of four fundamental concepts:

- Laying down rules before a negotiation

- Having a negotiation strategy based on SMARTnership

- Finding the Tru$tCurrency

- Focusing on NegoEconomics

LAYING DOWN THE RULES OF THE GAME BEFORE YOU START

There is some negotiation necessary before we even *start* a negotiation. This takes form in laying down some rules to guide how your negotiation will go.

Imagine you're on your way to a tennis match. Your racket is in your bag and you're looking forward to a good game of serve, rally, and volley. You're tremendously surprised when you arrive at the tennis court and your counterpart has set up two chairs and a table with a chessboard. He looks expectantly at you and says, "Are you ready to play?"

This scenario plays out every day in millions of cases worldwide, not literally with a tennis racket and a chessboard, but in a negotiation. One side comes to the table with an understanding of the rules of play and their opponent arrives with a completely different set of assumptions. Many of my clients over the years have been amazed when I open with the question: "Shall we talk about how we are going to negotiate?"

The first item of business in any negotiation, then, is for the parties to decide how they're going to negotiate. The Rules of the Game must be articulated and agreed to before any conversation takes places regarding the merits of the matter to be decided or the deal to be made. Who are the teams? What are the rules of play and the conditions for termination? This process can be time-consuming. In fact, it can sometimes take more time than the actual negotiation, but establishing the ground rules prior to bargaining saves a lot of time down the road, avoids misunderstandings, and enhances the prospects for cooperation.

The Rules of the Game must include an agreed agenda, the negotiation strategy, and agreement on the code of conduct:

- Should we negotiate in zero-sum, partnership, or SMARTnership?

- How do we divide the NegoEconomics value if we are negotiating in SMARTnership or partnership?

- Who will open the negotiation?

- Which parties will take a spot at the negotiation table?

- How do we establish trust?

- How do you present all variables? Who lists them?

- Who takes care of the whiteboard and visual aids?

- When and how often should we take breaks to regroup?

Failure to define the Rules of the Game is the same as showing up expecting a football game but finding a rugby game instead. Exciting game, but different set of rules than football.

The Negotiation Code of Conduct

This code establishes the rules of behavior that guide the company through even the most challenging situations. It includes statements of what employees engaging in negotiations on behalf of the company will and will not do in order to preserve the honesty and integrity of any negotiation, internally or externally. Every staff member in the organization should sign it, regardless of their position or role in the company.

In my business, I take this concept even further. Whenever I sit down at the table to negotiate with a trading partner, I ask them to sign it too. It sets the right climate for open communication and creates a positive environment.

I have developed a Negotiation Code of Conduct that can help you and your business partners establish rules of behavior to guide you through even the most challenging situations. Use my list as a basis for your own code of conduct, share it with your business partners, and reflect back on it when the stress levels rise:

We will not:

- Lie/bluff

- Intentionally put any pressure on the counterparty, including time pressure

- Make inflated offers

- Practice emotional manipulation

- Employ aggressive and hostile negotiation strategies and tactics

- Hold back information

We will:

- Put our best efforts to keep the trust level in negotiation as high as possible

- Restrain from spying, bribing, and infiltration attempts

- Keep our word if we reach an agreement

- Be open about variables and values and share the information on an equal level

- Try to observe fairness and even sharing of gained added value

We believe:

- That working together outperforms winning at the expense of the counterpart

- In the power of ethics and morality in negotiation

At the end of the day, openly adhering to a common set of moral and ethical guidelines buoys company morale while assuring your business partners that you are a fair dealer.

HAVING A NEGOTIATION STRATEGY BASED ON SMARTnership

Successful businesses have a strategy in place for virtually everything they do. They expend huge amounts of resources creating, developing, and fine-tuning a marketing strategy, a product development strategy, a human resources strategy, a communication strategy, and a research and development strategy. Can you imagine Apple or Toyota operating without defining these strategies or setting a budget? It's almost unthinkable.

I have asked this question about a negotiation strategy to countless audiences of business leaders of all cultures, generations, and genders—the results never change. Almost no one has a defined negotiation approach to govern how they transact business with their partners, suppliers, customers, or other stakeholders in their organization. The vast majority of negotiators have no strategic consciousness. They negotiate with their "gut" and allow emotions to drive their demands. Consequently, it becomes nearly impossible to develop open, honest, and transparent partnerships that allow for the creation of added value.

Why do you need a strategy? You must decide what you want from a trading partner to build a successful negotiation. Do you want a win-lose, zero-sum relationship that has few or no long-term prospects? Do you want a partnership where you share just enough to allow the relationship to function but keep enough distance so as not to reveal your hand? Or do you want a SMARTnership where you share your needs and desires in order to build a long-term relationship that can withstand the ups and downs inherent in commercial transactions? The result is that the concept of negotiation is envisioned very differently from delegate to delegate.

While collaboration is something many say they desire, many agreements end up in combative or zero-sum negotiations over and over again. Unfortunately, it is common for negotiators to lean toward aggressive tactics and only focus on winning—the irony being that they often lose (relationships, time, money) in doing so. Neither party benefits from an emotionally charged negotiation or zero-sum games. When rationality and confidence go out the window, so does the opportunity to leverage any value in your negotiation. That's why I'm a big proponent of using SMARTnership in negotiations.

In a SMARTnership relationship you need to be open, honest, and willing to cooperate at a different level than ever before. But that doesn't mean being naive! A naive negotiator gets punished and doesn't benefit from the value discovered. In this context, being naive means you are surrendering information without getting anything back. You should see a negotiation as a game of exchanging information. You'll need to work in SMARTnership with your counterpart in order to ensure getting a bigger slice of the pie.

A Successful SMARTnership Needs

- To operate from a position of mutual trust, honesty, and fair dealing

- To negotiate constructively, using open, transparent, two-way communication

- To leverage the differences between you and your counterpart

- To collaborate to reduce risk and improve the utilization of resources

These elements sound simple, but they make serious demands on the delegates and failure to follow them has enormous costs. According to studies I conducted with the Copenhagen Business School, businesses are forfeiting as much as 42 percent of the total value of the transaction because both sides fail to bargain for hidden variables— variables that may allow for an alternate solution that enhances the relative value of the transaction for both parties.[2]

Here's an example:

> Steve and Paige are doing a project together. They have been hired to build a wall. Steve's costs are $50 per yard, while Paige's are $30. If Paige builds the entire wall, the two of them will save $20 per yard. If Steve builds the entire wall, as opposed to sharing the task equally, they will save $10 per yard. By using SMARTnership they exchange the internal cost of building the wall, and by being open, transparent, and honest they quickly realize who should do the work.
>
> In a zero-sum game, there will be a disagreement about who is going to build the wall. The respective costs are often never shared openly and honestly. But if the partners collaborate in a SMARTnership fashion, they will leave the building to the party who can do the job at the lowest cost. Then the partners share the NegoEconomics generated, so that Paige is paid $35 per yard.

With a well-developed negotiation strategy, companies will find it easier to create relationships based on informed cooperation. By managing the personal chemistry and improving the flow of information, it becomes possible for two negotiators to achieve a relationship that makes problem solving more attractive than combat. This creates NegoEconomics, increases coinnovation, and allows for long-term stability in relationships.

FINDING THE Tru$tCurrency

The cornerstone of any SMARTnership—and the NegoEconomics doors it opens—is trust. Think of the trust factor like a cocktail, mixed with equal measures of trust, honesty, and cooperation; then flavored with the sincere intention that your negotiating counterpart will benefit handsomely from the deals you both concoct.

Negotiators enhance their business relationship's economic potential by seeking out opportunities for mutual gain. This is only successful where trust, honesty, transparency, fairness, and strong interest in mutual prosperity is the rule. When there is mutual agreement that these elements will govern interaction, information sharing, decision-making, and bargaining, a SMARTnership is formed. Through a SMARTnership, negotiation becomes creative and open, typically spawning far more bright new ideas and solutions than would ever be expected in traditional (adversarial) negotiation. Value is ultimately increased for both parties, and it's not uncommon for unforeseen benefits to extend far beyond the immediate environment of the participants. It all begins with the understanding that there are negotiation strategies beyond mere partnership and the zero-sum game.

This code of conduct is based on a set of values that determine particular rules of play:

- **Honesty:** There is a general understanding that a certain amount of bluffing is permitted in negotiations. Where that understanding originates, I don't know, but I often ask my clients if they ever lie in a negotiation; 49 percent admit they bluff occasionally. The common saying "If you tell the truth you don't have to remember anything" is so relevant when discussing honesty in negotiation. In order to capitalize on the potential of NegoEconomics, honesty is a basic requirement.

- **Full and fair disclosure:** In the opening of every negotiation in a SMARTnership, you'll need to negotiate how to negotiate.

That includes discussing the topic of full and fair disclosure. Should you share your cost and values with your counterpart? In order to achieve asymmetric value in your negotiation, you'll need to openly share your own values, otherwise you won't be able to identify the difference between your cost and the counterpart's values.

- **Respect for the dignity of the others:** I often quote my "golden rule" in negotiations. Don't ask for something that you wouldn't accept if the same were asked of you. Make sure your counterpart leaves the negotiation table feeling like a winner, instead of harboring resentment.

- **Ethics and morals:** Some years ago I met the CEO of a Fortune 500 company who shared his approach to ethics and morals. It was very simple. He said that if he was OK with a decision being on the front page of the business paper, he would go ahead with that decision. Another CEO I met said that before every important decision in his company, he thought about what his mom would feel about the decision. If she would be OK with it, he would go ahead with the decision. Having a code of conduct to guide you through a negotiation is an essential component of every negotiation.

FOCUSING ON NegoEconomics

Think back to the pizza example in the Introduction. A transaction can be thought of as slices in a pizza pie. Two parties can divide a small pizza equally or they might agree to some other ratio, say one-third or two-thirds of the pie. But when both parties mutually pursue the additional value in the deal, then the pizza becomes larger, and both can net more than the value of their original half and get more slices to satisfy their hunger.

NegoEconomics is the active pursuit of that additional value through cooperative deal-making. In other words, a mutual effort to increase the size of the pie and expand the room for negotiation. The added—or asymmetric—value that results from NegoEconomics comes in many forms, such as more money, reduced competition, increased inventory, additional intellectual capital, or improved brand awareness. Once the asymmetric value has been located, all that remains to negotiate is how to divide it.

For example, Paul is a manufacturing supplier running a small company with very little cash on hand. He is signing a $10 million contract with a manufacturing company named UniTec. UniTec's negotiators want to pay him at the time of delivery, which is six months in the future. This puts Paul in a difficult situation. His subsuppliers, on whom he depends to be able to fulfill the UniTec order, are demanding up-front payment to deliver the parts he needs. The subsuppliers all require 30 percent up front on the total order value, which adds up to $3 million. This is money Paul doesn't have.

Paul has two options:

1. He can go to his bank and ask them for a loan for $3 million.

2. He can ask UniTec if they will pay $3 million up front.

He opts for option 2. UniTec's lead negotiator tells Paul that the up-front payment is out of the question and adds that if he requires it, the negotiator will cancel the contract and search for an alternative supplier.

Paul's only remaining alternative is to approach his bank for a loan. The bank approves the loan but charges him $150,000 interest. This, of course, reduces his profit on the deal by $150,000.

Let's say UniTec's cost of paying Paul the $3 million up front is $60,000. The reason? Their cost of capital is lower than Paul's.

UniTec's negotiator believes he won a strategic victory by not paying Paul anything up front. Paul knows he did not handle this negotiation well, but in reality both parties lost. Both lost the potential of creating NegoEconomic value by leveraging the terms of payment variable—in this case, the difference between Paul's cost and UniTec's gains:

What should Paul and UniTec have done instead? By figuring out the difference between their respective costs of capital, they would easily have discovered that by utilizing this difference they created $90,000 of NegoEconomics to divide between them. Imagine if Paul reduced his price by $120,000—UniTec would make an additional $60,000 and Paul would save $30,000. A win for everybody (with the exception of the bank, which is not part of the deal).

The objective of NegoEconomics is to establish a creative and constructive dialogue that will improve the conditions for finding a distribution acceptable to both parties. The sharing of the value does not need to be a 50–50 split. One party might take the whole amount of the value. Or the split could be 90–10, which would be within the spirit of SMARTnership if the party receiving 10 percent is satisfied with the outcome. NegoEconomics often means distributing tasks to the party who can perform the function at the lowest cost. If one side's costs are higher than the other side's, the task is allocated to the party who has the lowest cost ownership.

ESSENTIAL TAKEAWAYS

- You succeed in negotiation by following four fundamental concepts: setting the Rules of the Game, using SMARTnerships as your negotiation strategy, understanding the financial consequences of Tru$tCurrency, and focusing on NegoEconomics.

- When you create a bigger pie, there's more to share.

- Always define your negotiation strategy when starting a negotiation.

- NegoEconomics generates added value.

CHAPTER

11

How to Negotiate Effectively Using NegoEconomics

Regardless of your job, career, or industry, the ability to negotiate *effectively* is crucial. That fact may surprise you—or it might just confirm what you've thought all along. Of all other skills essential to success, including critical thinking, managing people, dealing with complex problems, and coordinating with others, being an effective negotiator is rapidly growing in popularity as a skill to be carefully cultivated. The World Economic Forum has placed negotiation as one of the 15 *most* important skills for attaining success in any job or function.[1] Additionally, a recent study conducted by the speaker's agency Speakers Gold ranked "negotiation" on their list of the 25 most popular keynote topics in North America.[2]

Every week, I encounter professionals in a variety of fields and industries who routinely negotiate in their work—some for contracts valued in the many millions—without any formal training or theoretical background in negotiation. They learned by simply doing it, through raw experience, and by observing colleagues and others. I know some who claim to have 20 years or more of such negotiating experience. I'd estimate, though, that in reality they have the equivalent of one year's experience, copied 20 times over. But whether they have 1 or 20 years of experience under their belts, I can say for sure there is no such thing as a "born negotiator," despite the popular belief in such mythical creatures. You have to learn and practice how to be a negotiator. And not just any negotiator—an *effective* negotiator.

USING NegoEconomics TO CAPITALIZE ON POTENTIAL

One key part in being good at negotiation is knowing how to capitalize on potential. Our studies have showed that up to 42 percent of the potential values that could be created in a negotiation are never identified, capitalized on, or utilized by the parties involved.[3] Those unidentified values are a result of the asymmetric differences between the parties' costs and benefits connected with each negotiated variable. That's where NegoEconomics comes in. NegoEconomics is the act of generating value on both sides of the negotiation table. Negotiation methods can be divided into two main categories: zero-sum games and collaborations. As discussed in previous chapters, in a zero-sum negotiation there is only one result in negotiating—you win at the expense of the counterpart or the counterpart wins at your expense.

As an example, let's say you're negotiating transportation costs with your client. You know your cost of transportation in the transaction would be $20,000. But you have no clue what your counterpart's costs would be for transporting the same goods. Your counterpart is keeping that number close to his chest as an advantage, expecting you to throw out the first number and potentially use it to offer a lower number than your counterpart originally planned. You also decide to not reveal your cost, creating a zero-sum approach: neither you nor your counterpart are willing to give the other the upper hand to come to an agreement that would benefit both of you.

Meanwhile, a collaboration is exactly what it sounds like—two parties work together, build trust, and establish relationships to create a beneficial result. Collaboration can be further divided into two subcategories: partnerships and SMARTnerships. In a partnership, the parties attempt to create progress without causing a loss for the counterpart but are not necessarily open and trusting. In a SMARTnership, openness, rules of the game, and trust have been agreed to and verbalized prior to beginning actual negotiations. Going back to our transport cost example, you tell your counterpart your transportation cost would be $20,000; your counterpart then shares that his or her cost for the same transportation would be only $15,000. In this way, you would have discovered a potential *and negotiable* value of $5,000.

USING ZERO-SUM GAMES IN NEGOTIATION

Deciding when to use zero-sum negotiation and when to collaborate depends a lot on the circumstances at hand. You use collaboration primarily to establish relationships, build trust, and create Nego-Economics. A collaboration will more likely lead to a less contentious and negative negotiation. In zero-sum games, you either focus on winning at the expense of the counterpart or you try to dissolve a previous negotiation built through collaboration.

There might be negotiations where we purposely need to embrace a zero-sum approach. For example, if we are forced to negotiate with the counterpart but they don't want to collaborate—forcing us into a positional negotiation. Zero-sum negotiations typically lead to solutions with winners and losers, or solutions in which *both* parties lose. Alternative paths to the terms and values on the negotiation table are rarely considered in these situations.

Imagine the opposing parties are in their respective trenches, pointing rifles at each other. There is an absolute lack of communication, trust, and transparency. As a result, NegoEconomics values are never identified and realized.

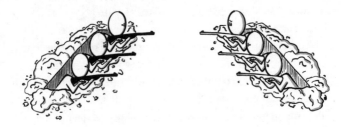

In zero-sum negotiations, it's typical for the process to center around a solution that has been a given from the outset. Remember the pizza analogy in the Introduction? Discussion in zero-sum negotiations is centered around a pizza of a predetermined size, which is to be divided between the negotiating parties. The more slices that go to the other party, the less slices you get. Any gain for one party is at the expense of the other.

Zero-sum negotiation techniques include bluffs, threats, and play-acting. The participants behave as though they are negotiating a hostage situation, where only one party can walk away a winner. In various ways, each party attempts to force the other to make concessions. While it seems like one party always wins in this method, anything won in this way typically costs more than it is worth.

Here's an example. A supplier requests the buyer pay an advance of $100,000. The buyer claims that none of the other suppliers approached has asked for an advance. He goes so far as to add, "Our policy is never to pay advances. If you persist in your demand, the deal will not happen." The supplier—not especially clever as a negotiator and operating within a rigidly limited framework—concedes. As a result, he loses $100,000.

How much does the buyer really gain by shutting down the deal? Let's assume his interest costs are somewhat lower than the supplier's, so that in reality it would only cost $70,000 to make the advance payment. In this zero-sum game, the parties lose $30,000. The difference between the supplier's value of $100,000 compared to the buyer's cost of $70,000. The $30,000 is the NegoEconomics of the deal—the asymmetric value between the two parties' cost and value.

Through more skillful negotiation, the value of $100,000 from the advance payment the seller conceded might have been utilized in another way, yielding greater gains for the buyer. A better solution for both parties might have been a unilateral price reduction of $80,000, if the supplier would get the payment in advance. This would have meant only an additional $10,000 for the buyer (remember that his actual cost would've been only $70,000), while the supplier would only lose $20,000 instead of $100,000. There might have been even better options available to the seller. He might have been able to include a year of free service—a greater value to the buyer than better payment conditions.

Unfortunately, when taking a zero-sum approach, it's typical for negotiators to work with unnecessarily costly solutions. Resources disappear into thin air, and neither party has a share in them. Further, zero-sum games spawn a negative negotiating climate, resulting in mutual distrust and lack of openness.

A lack of openness means that when the negotiators are deciding on the terms they'll ask for, or which they're willing to accept, they only look at the consequences to themselves. They do not have, nor have they attempted to obtain, information about the consequences of their terms and conditions to the other party. This yields less-optimum results because potential rationalizations and more advantageous cost distributions may be missed. Some sellers, facing similar buyer demands, might stiffen their defenses. To continue our example, the supplier could call the buyer's bluff and raise a counterargument: "Nowadays, everybody asks for an advance. If we don't get one, we have to raise our prices. And in all our past transactions, you've accepted paying an advance."

A solution to this type of verbal combat could be a reduction of the advance from $100,000 to $90,000 or $80,000. The parties still have a loss to share, albeit a smaller one. Plus, they run the risk of getting stuck in counteroffers and arguments as each side attempts to gain the upper hand, which ultimately erodes trust in the business relationship.

Instead of seeing demands like in the example as threats, look at them as opportunities that can be used to yield NegoEconomics. To determine whether such opportunities exist, you'll have to engage your counterpart in a constructive dialogue.

USING COLLABORATION INSTEAD IN YOUR NEGOTIATIONS

A systematic search for NegoEconomics can often yield new solutions that better serve both parties' needs and requirements. If there is a bigger pizza to be shared, the parties are more likely to find a division acceptable to both. And they may end up forming a partnership in which both are well satisfied, and neither need relinquish anything significant in arriving at a sound agreement. Both sides enjoy success—and not at the expense of either, as in a zero-sum game.

Successful negotiating means doing a thorough, unbiased review of the existing alternatives. If you want to locate better solutions than those immediately at hand, or obtain additional information about your counterpart's requirements, take the approach I refer to as collaborative partnership. It's characterized by constructive dialogue and a foundation of trust and openness.

In the case described earlier, the seller could have replied, "The interest gain we'd obtain against the advance will benefit you by way of a lower price. We can certainly look at the financing aspects and the amount of the advance, but that will affect the price."

Here the seller keeps the door open for discussion. The buyer listens, then asks, "How much is the advance worth to you?" Now the need for openness and honesty comes into play. Will the seller be open and honest and reply, "Around $100,000"? If so, the buyer knows how cost-intensive his demand is. He can relate the extra cost of the $100,000 advance to his gain of $70,000. He can see that it eats up more than it yields, and he can try to discover whether other requirements might give a better yield. He sees the opportunity and exploits the difference between the parties' interest costs by offering a higher advance if he can get a share of the NegoEconomics thus accruing. "We could raise the advance by 50 percent, but then you would have to come down by . . ."

The Flipside to Collaboration

I have known many companies that claim they are in partnership with their suppliers and clients. After carefully analyzing their contract and negotiation process, I often conclude that these companies are not in a partnership but are instead in a long-term zero-sum game.

A true partnership requires certain building blocks. The parties are aware of the potential that lies in NegoEconomics. They have established some form of trust and transparency but often lack the rules of the game or an agreed code of conduct. Instead of two trenches of soldiers pointing guns at each other, a partnership can be visualized as a round trench with all soldiers in it. Communication is certainly better than in a zero-sum negotiation, and openness and trust might have improved as well, but the rifles are still pointing toward each other. In many cases, one party is still winning at the expense of the counterpart.

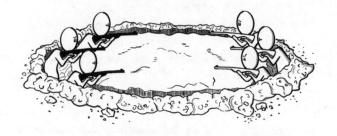

Many negotiators find it difficult to get a good, functioning collaboration going. They have insufficient insight into the advantages that can be realized, and they aren't well motivated to instigate or build cooperation. They aren't conscious of the demands the cooperative approach makes on them or on their negotiating partners. They are unable to initiate an open, constructive dialogue, which is a requirement to making a cooperative negotiation work.

Such negotiators find themselves emotionally affected by situations that arise in a negotiation. Perceived threats, feelings of insecurity, and other stressors trigger their emotions, sorely diminishing their ability to remain rational. Their automatic response is to counter with a knee-jerk, fight-or-flight reaction.

Since I recognized that so many negotiators and organizations worldwide often misunderstand or abuse the word *partnership*, I developed partnership version 2.0, or as we call it, SMARTnership. SMARTnership requires the tools I share with you in this book. The negotiators join forces in a circular trench, with everyone aiming for maximum mutual benefits through transparent, honest, and open negotiations. If cost cuts can be found, improving on the original bid, both parties split the value of the savings.

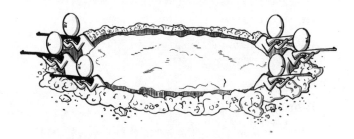

HOW OUR SUBCONSCIOUS MOTIVES ENDANGER NEGOTIATION

We typically lack insight into our own needs and desires, both conscious and subconscious. This can lead to conflicts in our interactions with others (which we blame on the other person) not only in our personal lives but also in our business relationships. Only when we become aware of these mechanisms and learn to see the link between their subconscious effects and our outward actions can we attain the maturity required to tackle certain types of interactions.

For example, a woman is cooking dinner but discovers she forgot to buy cream. She asks her husband, who is watching sports on the TV, to go to the store for some cream. He now faces an internal conflict: he doesn't really want to leave his comfortable chair but he also wants to meet his wife's wishes. He is someone who does whatever he can to avoid conflicts, or at least postpone them, so he agrees to the trip. The grocery store is five minutes away, but a full hour passes before the husband is back. His wife is very annoyed:

> **Wife:** Where have you been? I've been waiting and waiting, and our dinner is all but ruined.
>
> **Husband:** First I went to the grocery store, but they wanted $4 for the cream. I know it's only $2.50 at the minimart.
>
> **Wife:** So, you drove all the way to the minimart—another three miles—to save $1.50?
>
> **Husband:** I don't think it's fair, the way they try to take advantage of the customers at the grocery store.
>
> **Wife:** I'm sure you only did it to annoy me. You were mad because I made you leave your television, but you're always too cowardly tell me straight-out!

Does the husband realize that he did what he did to get even with his wife? He isn't willing to admit his motive and denies his wife's assertion. He feels he is being treated unfairly—after all, he *did* sacrifice his TV program to get the cream his wife had forgotten to buy.

Although most of us try to stand on firm ground, making decisions and acting only after collecting and assessing facts, there are always subconscious and repressed needs, motives, fears, and hopes lurking in the background and coloring our decisions. In fact, we are governed by them. It's important to become aware of these subconscious factors—to become aware of our own desires, intentions, and emotions and how they come into play in day-to-day life. By becoming more conscious of our impulses, we learn to better control them.

If you lack insight into how your own behavior, choice of approach, language, and ability to communicate vary and are governed in different situations, how can the party across the table be expected to understand, predict, and react appropriately to your signals and decisions?

In the field of negotiation technique, there is no such thing as absolute truth. Nor is there any list of invariably correct actions and results, in which two plus two always equals four.

You should learn and practice several approaches and view them as strings on a violin—a tool with which you can create a variety of chords. Train your "musical ear" to be responsive to any situation so that harmonious resonance can arise between you and the other members of the orchestra.

CHOOSING STRATEGIES AND TACTICS

Deciding which strategy (zero-sum, partnership, or SMARTnership) and tactics you'll follow is one of the most important elements of negotiation preparation. If you don't work out your strategy and tactics ahead of time, you hand the other party the initiative and force yourself to negotiate on their terms and conditions. These will impact your attitude, decisions, and behavior throughout the negotiation. Tactics are the individual moves you employ while negotiating. The Strategy Assessment Matrix model was created to help you identify the correct negotiation strategy based on the parties' importance to each other.

Strategy Assessment Matrix

The vertical line indicates how important you are to the counterpart. The more important you are, the higher they will place you on the vertical line. The horizontal line indicates how important the counterpart is to you. The more important they are, the further you'll place them toward the right. If both parties find each other equally important, we'll end up in the top right box. What is the right negotiation strategy in the top right box? Zero-sum, partnership, or SMARTnership? I hope you said SMARTnership.

On the other hand, if you are not important to the counterpart and the counterpart is not really important to you, you are in the bottom left box. What is the chosen strategy in that box? Zero-sum. It doesn't make sense to invest time or resources engaging in SMARTnership in that case, since you don't find value in your counterpart. In an unbalanced negotiation, where one party is more important than the counterpart, you'll find yourself in either the top left corner or bottom right corner, in which case partnership should be implemented.

Here are some of the things that could influence what strategy you choose when you engage in negotiations:

- Your choice of strategy can be, to an extent, a product of your personal upbringing and even your heredity. Further, the behavior you demonstrate in business negotiations is typically very much in keeping with your behavior vis-à-vis your family members, neighbors, and colleagues.

- Your strategy selection can also be affected by your expectations regarding a negotiation. If you believe the other party will be quite aggressive and spoiling for a fight, you may well favor a fight yourself, without examining whether another strategy might be better suited to the purpose, or whether a fight is even likely to take you to your goal. The inverse is also true. If the other party appears to be willing to cooperate, you're likely to lean toward cooperation yourself.

- Your organization's policies and general view of the surrounding world affect your choice of strategy. A negotiator adjusts his or her behavior to the perceived expectations of the organization and its managers.

There are negotiators who are aware of the importance of strategy choice. Before any negotiation begins, they very deliberately plan a strategy and how they will implement it. They always consider the topical negotiation situation. They know how to vary their strategy when needed, and how to shift to a completely new strategy when necessary. They see a negotiation as consisting of two steps:

1. Creating NegoEconomics

2. Then dividing the NegoEconomics values

Their behavior at the negotiating table is governed by goal-oriented planning and a feeling for how their own behavior and reactions to the other party's moves can bring them closer to their objectives. They've developed their own register of emotions and are sensitive to the many facets of human interaction. They avoid all types of verbal combat, provocation, locks, and prestige-oriented conflicts that aren't part of a well-designed and executed negotiation.

There is no such thing as a general tactic that will work no matter the circumstances. Tactics must always be adjusted and adapted to your objectives, strategy, resources, and knowledge—as well as the other party's objectives, strategy, resources, and knowledge.

Some tactics are constructive, leading to greater openness and enhanced understanding. They foster trust. Using such tactics makes it easier to find paths that will lead you to NegoEconomics. However, many of the tactical plays negotiators use try to manipulate the other party, making them feel insecure and exerting pressure that may become overwhelming. Such stressful moves may seem efficient in the short term—but they tend to ruin relationships, trust, and openness. There are negotiation situations in which cooperation between the parties works well, making tactical, "clever" moves superfluous and sure to do more harm than good.

Sometimes it's difficult to determine in advance whether one tactic will prove superior to another, or whether clever gambits and moves will be harmful, not beneficial. Only when the negotiation is over will you know the outcome. But you'll never know what the outcome might have been, had you chosen another strategy.

A good working principle in tactic choice is to begin with gambits that won't lock the negotiation and limit the possibility of taking a different route at a later stage. Try to design a negotiation with a view to cooperation from the outset. If you're uncertain about the other party's intentions, take it easy and wait until you can get a reliable read on them. Be wary of any gambit the other party might interpret as combative. Such gambits can easily lead to a deadlocked negotiation and preempt future cooperation.

Double-Edged Tactics

Tactical moves must be made with good sense and caution. Clever tactics tend to be two-edged swords. If the other party sees through your intentions, a clever countermove may still put that party where you want him or her. Negotiations are reminiscent of chess. Just like the chess player, the skillful negotiator is always several moves ahead of the opponent.

Never use a tactic without having a clear idea what reactions and countermoves it might provoke, and how you would handle them. Put yourself in your counterpart's shoes; consider how that person might react and countermove, faced with the moves you have in mind. If you're smart about this, you can avoid ruining relations and openness. When you're testing boundaries and positions, be firm, stick to your guns, and express your demands—without resorting to combative moves.

It's the rule rather than the exception that negotiations are full of surprises. It quite often becomes clear when your initial picture of a negotiation was incomplete and partially wrong. Be responsive and flexible, ready to adjust to the reality that greets you at the negotiating table. Unfortunately, many negotiators are inflexible. Instead of making agile adjustments, they try to force reality to fit their negotiation design. If negotiations are slipping from your grip, *take a break!*

I'm a staunch believer in cooperation. Cooperation is based upon trust, open and honest communication, and a willingness to listen and understand each other's needs and judgments. Cooperation in no way means skirting real issues or abandoning your own needs and judgments. The purpose is to make the stake as large as possible, to the benefit of both parties.

THE LION KING AND NEGOTIATION STYLES: WHAT CAN WE LEARN?

Disney's classic animated movie *The Lion King* is not just a story about a young lion named Simba trying to reclaim his rightful place as king of the Pride Lands. It's also a tale of negotiation and conflict. If we look closely, we can identify several negotiation styles and stereotypes among the characters in the movie.

The first style we can identify is SMARTnership, a style of negotiation where parties work together to create a win-win situation. In the movie, this style is used when Simba and Nala team up to search for food in the elephant graveyard.

The manipulative combative negotiation style involves aggressive and confrontational tactics. Scar, the villain of the movie, uses this style to manipulate the hyenas into doing his bidding. It involves using deceptive tactics to gain an advantage. Scar employs this style throughout the movie, most notably when he convinces Simba that his father's death was his fault.

Compromise, where both parties give up something to reach a mutually beneficial agreement, is shown when Mufasa agrees to let Scar stay in the Pride Lands despite his disapproval.

The zero-sum approach is where parties focus solely on maximizing their own gains. The hyenas use this style, hoping to gain access to the Pride Lands in exchange for their loyalty to Scar.

Partnership, where parties work together toward a common goal, is seen when Simba, Timon, and Pumbaa join forces to protect the Pride Lands. And it is often seen from Sarabi as well, when she works with Nala to fight off Scar.

The notetaker is a neutral mediator used by negotiating parties to facilitate the negotiation process. Often, this is the member of the negotiation team that notes details in the negotiation. Zazu is a notetaker; he uses his skill to take note of what is happening across the Pride Lands and report back to Mufasa.

The next style is stalling, where parties delay negotiations to gain more time to prepare or to weaken the other party's position. Scar uses this style when he continuously promises the hyenas they will have freedom and power once he becomes king—a feat that keeps being delayed.

Concession is where one party gives in to the other's demands to reach an agreement. Simba gives up his Hakuna Matata lifestyle when he decides to return to the Pride Lands and confront Scar, after pressure from Nala to restore order and justice to the kingdom.

As we can see, negotiation shows up even where we least expect it—in our children's stories. By analyzing the different negotiation styles and techniques used by the characters of *The Lion King*, we can learn valuable lessons about real-life negotiation. The movie serves as a great tool for educators and negotiators to help illustrate the right and wrong ways to negotiate. The next time you watch *The Lion King*, keep an eye out for these negotiation styles and see what you can learn from them.

ESSENTIAL TAKEAWAYS

- There is no such thing as a born negotiator. Just as with anything in life, the more you study and practice negotiating, the better you'll be at it.

- You can choose to negotiate in a zero-sum or a collaborative way.

- NegoEconomics can normally only be realized in a SMARTnership negotiation.

- Always use breaks in your negotiations.

- Discuss rules of the game (how to negotiate), trust, and transparency even before beginning the actual negotiation.

NegoEconomics
in Action

We can now put everything we've learned so far in this book to use. Let's look at an example that shows NegoEconomics in action.

A box manufacturer and a lid supplier have been doing business together for six years. They work together well. The supplier produces a perfectly sized and secure lid for the type of small box the manufacturer makes. The total value of the past year's transactions between the two parties was $25 million.

In the annual negotiation meeting between the supplier and manufacturer, the supplier is pleased to say that there will be no price increase in the coming year. However, the manufacturer explains that the price they have been paying is too high. If the supplier's price cannot be reduced by 9 percent, the manufacturer will have to accept an alternative bid by a competitor who also makes lids the size they need. The total cost reduction the manufacturer seeks is $2,250,000.

This demand takes the supplier completely by surprise; he was not prepared for such a development. They have worked together without issues for the past six years. The supplier asks for a break to consider the demand.

Instead of looking at simply granting the discount (which would be a unilateral concession), the supplier looks for other elements and variables in their overall value chain that could be negotiated, thereby generating NegoEconomics—opportunities for both sides to benefit from continuing the relationship. The supplier takes a look at their existing agreement with the manufacturer. The terms are:

- Delivery is handled by the supplier, serving 16 different geographical locations.

- Delivery takes place every week.

- Warehousing of the product is managed by the supplier.

- The supplier produces and delivers the product on a just-in-time, or only as they're needed, basis.

- The supplier covers the product with a three-year warranty.

- Payment terms are net 65 days after delivery.

Having reviewed the existing terms, the supplier requests a new meeting to explore common costs and potential savings. The supplier expresses their willingness to be open, if the manufacturer is similarly willing. The manufacturer agrees, and the meeting is held. The parties isolate the following costs and potential savings:

- The supplier's additional cost (gas, trucks, driver salaries, etc.) for supplying 16 different locations (rather than a single location) on a just-in-time basis is $580,000.

- Monthly deliveries, rather than weekly, would save the supplier $260,000 over the course of a year.

- Storing the products costs the supplier $618,000/year in warehouse costs.

- The supplier's cost for the three-year warranty is $310,000 more than for a one-year warranty.

- The supplier's interest costs are 7 percent annually.

- Just-in-time production (rather than periodic bulk production) costs the supplier an additional $675,000 annually.

- By modifying the size of the product, the supplier could save $2,400,000 annually.

After making their own calculations, the manufacturer concludes:

- The manufacturer's costs would increase by $140,000 if shipments were received at a single location, rather than 16.

- The customer's costs would increase by $80,000 if delivery was once a month, rather than once a week, to optimize logistics (since they receive the product less frequently).

- Storing the product on location rather than the supplier's warehouse would increase the customer's costs by $160,000.

- Decreasing the warranty period from three years to one year would increase the customer's costs by $125,000.

- The manufacturer's interest rate is 3 percent.

- If the supplier shifted from just-in-time production to periodic production, it would cost the customer an additional $210,000.

- Changing the size of the product would cost the customer $820,000.

With all the variables they've laid out, the business pair fill out their planner:

Variable	Supplier	Manufacturer	Room for Negotiation
Delivery 16 locations to 1	-580,000	-140,000	+440,000
Delivery once a month	+260,000	-80,000	+180,000
Warehousing	-618,000	-160,000	+458,000
Warranty 3 years	-310,000	+125,000	-185,000
Interest rate	7%	3%	4% (890,000)
Just-in-time	+675,000	+210,000	+885,000
Change of product format	+2,400,000	-820,000	+1,580,000
Total NegoEconomics			=4,248,000

Imagine you are one of the parties in this negotiation. You are sitting at the table, looking at the pile of money you'll have created with your counterpart: $4,248,000. How should you split the NegoEconomics?

Let's take a look at our options:

- Agree on the distribution in advance and how possible savings are to be divided among the parties before starting to look for new solutions. "Let us share the amount saved so that you get 60 percent and we, as suppliers, settle for 40 percent."

- Try to find a distribution scale both parties consider fair. It could be divided based on which party has the most costs or risks, who puts in the most effort, which company is most profitable or larger, and so on. Experience shows, however, that the assessment of your own and the opponent's efforts is sensitive. Many negotiations fail because the parties get stuck in an assessment conflict where they unintentionally insult each other by exaggerating their own value and downgrading the opponent's, which negatively impacts interpersonal and business relationships.

- The parties demand full compensation for their increased costs and exaggerate on their invoices. "To manufacture and pack the products in this new way increases our costs from X to Z." Because you focus the arguments on your own loss, you only run a small risk of ending up in an assessment conflict.

- Take advantage of the competitive situation. "We just reduced your Total Cost of Ownership by X."

- Work toward a prearranged goal. "If we can present a solution where we have squeezed the costs down from $25 million today to $22.5 million, then the order is ours."

- Try to gain insight into the opponent's calculation. Give them reasonable compensation for all the increased costs and a modest earnings improvement. The rest of the pie is yours.

- Go over the other party's head. Show the supplier's proposition to the competitor, if there is one, and tell the competitor how they can improve their bid by going below the supplier's bid. I don't recommend this method, but it is something you may encounter if you deal with cheap business relations where the short-term gains are more important than good relations and a good reputation.

The two parties ended up creating a mutual value of $4,248,000. The buyer got the requested $2,250,000 and the two parties shared the difference between $4,248,000 and $2,250,000, which resulted in the supplier even optimizing their financial outcome of the negotiation by $974,000.

HOW LONG WILL OUR COOPERATION LAST?

Can the lid manufacturer now lean back and earn a lot of money just by setting a new process, changing the variables, and using NegoEconomics? No. The competitors will copy their method. Other production methods and materials will be developed to outsell the products. The new manufacturing method can be exported to a country with lower prices and knock the existing supplier out. A forward-looking supplier can initiate this development and control it.

Those who fail to be open to negotiating will have a difficult time in today's open market. Buyers can no longer afford to be loyal to one place. A frequent flyer, once loyal to one airline, is driven by rising airfare costs to explore and start loyalty programs with other airlines, for example. There is no buyer who can afford to keep buying in one place solely because of loyalty.

As seen in this scenario, the market situation and competition increase the pressure on the need to create and maintain competitive advantages. Increased global competition also increases the pressure on companies with respect to rationalization and new development.

The only way to win in this changing market is by helping each other.

ESSENTIAL TAKEAWAYS

- Revisit existing agreements and look for variables that could generate asymmetric values.

- A contract is never final. If both parties are willing to renegotiate, it's negotiable.

- Price is far from the only variable that should be negotiated.

- We often negotiate on too few variables. Expand the number of variables before negotiating.

- The best method toward creating NegoEconomics is to agree on how to split the pie before value has been capitalized.

CHAPTER

13

The Ongoing Journey of Negotiation

What motivates you to succeed? This is the question I often ask when meeting other professionals for the first time. Throughout my career, people have always been somewhat taken back by the question. After they get over their initial surprise, they proceed to add to the endless assortment of responses I've heard, such as family, career success, freedom, boating, and even horse-riding music. Yes, that's right—horse-riding music.

Regardless of the plethora of answers, the primary stories that dominate media headlines focus on money and power as motivators to succeed in life. Human beings are naturally fascinated by these particular motivators, fixated on the lives and stories of celebrities, influential politicians, and business leaders. Their vast sums of money astonish the public, as do the lifestyles that come with it. We watch their interviews, read their articles, and use the products they endorse in hopes that doing so will provide the secret formula for professional and financial success.

For the more traditional careers that apply to 99 percent of us, I believe there is one key skill required to achieve the money or power of the 1 percent. Consider what abilities would be most valuable if your task was to convince your boss to give you a pay raise. If you are in a discussion with a valuable client, what skills are necessary to retain the account or create favorable terms? In your personal life, how would you increase your travel budget when your partner is against it, obtain a refund after the warranty expired, or make an appeal to the most attractive person you've ever met to go on a first date with you? Your success in all these situations is dependent on your ability to negotiate.

Yes, you read correctly. If you want power, money, or influence, you must negotiate. Negotiation is not just for *Shark Tank* contestants. Anytime you are trying to generate a favorable outcome with another individual or party, you negotiate. As Dale Carnegie famously stated in his bestselling book *How to Win Friends and Influence People*, "Even in such technical lines as engineering, about 15% of one's financial success is due to one's technical knowledge and about 85% is due to skill in human engineering, to personality and the ability to lead people."[1] Human engineering is your ability to influence yourself and others.

Henry Kissinger, former political scientist and diplomat, is perhaps one of the most iconic examples of a man whose negotiation skills helped him achieve it all. Kissinger rose from a young boy fleeing Nazi Germany for the United States to a Harvard student and professor, to National Security Advisor to Secretary of the State under President Richard Nixon, and finally to *TIME* magazine's "Man of the Year." He climbed the ranks with nothing but sheer determination and an incredible ability to persuade. While a truly controversial figure, he is renowned for helping to end the Vietnam War and bringing the prisoners of war home, for meeting face-to-face with the leaders of China to establish diplomatic relations, and for personally negotiating the end of conflict between Egypt and Israel. By leveraging his skill, he put himself in a position of power and then wielded it to create more power.

It's hard to deny the potent effects of money and influence but even harder to avoid the fact that negotiation is the superpower of the professional elite. Top negotiators not only sway the ideas of others, but they are masters at building rapport and a spirit of cooperation and collaboration. They also know when to assert themselves and take control. In traditional careers, the ability to negotiate is the key to money and power—but always remember to be careful what you wish for. These aspects don't guarantee fulfillment or true happiness.

BECOME THE BEST NEGOTIATOR YOU CAN BE

A bad negotiation can be compared to driving a nail into a wall. It can be done just with one blow, but it takes time to pull the nail out again and it cannot be done without leaving a mark where the nail was. You can use strategies that seem good in the moment but are detrimental to your cause, ruin interpersonal relationships by not being honest or respectful, or even not show up prepared to the negotiation table. And I guarantee all those things widen that hole in the wall.

The examples and experiences in this book show that negotiation is a high-stakes psychological game—a game professionals and nonprofessionals play against one another in everyday situations.

Sometimes it is against opponents we know, and sometimes against opponents we don't know. But do you know yourself? Do you know how you react to pressure or to combativeness?

To be better at negotiating, start with knowing yourself. Dare stare your own skills, and faults, in the eyes. You can't change your opponents; they are who they are. It is your own behavior you must get to know, develop, and change. If you are sympathetic, open, and adaptable, you'll find negotiating will come easier to you.

Even though every negotiation is unique and calls for its own solutions, there is a lot you can learn from other people, trades, and situations. Be open to discussion—it is not dangerous to get to know one another better, gain respect for one another, and explore and divulge new information. As a skilled negotiator, you'll know that it becomes much easier to reach an agreement if you can create added values that can be distributed to both yourself and your negotiating counterpart. This book describes a number of negotiation tools that will help you succeed. But if you try to make the negotiation into a game where you constantly try to outdo, fight, or take advantage of your opponent—well, then I've failed in getting my message across.

On the other hand, if you choose to negotiate with strength and grace for your counterpart, you'll gain much in return—not only in winning a negotiation but in building interpersonal relationships that can lead you into the next positive negotiation. This book is about winning negotiations, but not at all costs. If there's anything you should take from this book, it is that negotiation requires both give *and* take, not just take.

Use the tools in this book to train yourself for negotiations and gain experience by doing more of them. My examples throughout show how much can be learned from the negotiations we participate in every day.

I wish you good luck with your negotiations and the creation of NegoEconomics via the SMARTnership concept. If you want to further pursue becoming an exceptional negotiator, I have various online resources available to facilitate your ongoing learning. These tools can be found at www.smartnershipclass.com.

If you have comments on or questions about this book, you are most welcome to contact me by email: keld@keldjensen.com.

Negotiation
Essentials Toolkit

To help maximize the knowledge you gained from this book, I want to provide you with resources to support your development as a negotiator. These components include:

- The Dos and Don'ts of Negotiation

- Prenegotiation Checklist

- Postnegotiation Evaluation Checklist

- SMARTnership Negotiation Quiz

THE DOS AND DON'TS OF NEGOTIATION

Dos

- Make sure to prepare before a negotiation. Use the negotiation planner and checklists as tools, and create an agenda before entering the negotiation room.

- If you work in a team, have a leader, notetaker, and calculator.

- Ask questions instead of arguing.

- Listen to what the counterpart is really saying.

- Know your starting point, threshold of pain, and target goal in a negotiation.

- Learn how to identify when a negotiation is occurring.

- Identify your negotiation strategy: zero-sum, partnership, or SMARTnership.

- List and value your variables.

- Try to expand the number of variables, preferably with your counterpart.

- Create and develop trust.

- Be sure to negotiate with a counterpart who has authority to sign a deal.

- Use breaks during negotiations.

- Summarize what you have discussed during negotiation.

- Identify the negotiation style of your counterpart.

- Use visual aids.

Dont's

- Negotiate price as the first or only variable.

- Use ultimatums.

- Negotiate on your own without a team, unless it's a simple negotiation.

- Ignore the value in face-to-face negotiations versus virtual negotiations.

- Give something away without getting something in return.

- Accept your counterpart dictating the terms or agenda.

- Begin a negotiation without proper preparation.

- Make final decisions without a break.

- Ask closed-ended questions in the beginning of a negotiation.

- Assume you know the culture of your counterpart.

- Assume or guess what the counterparts wants.

- Put yourself under time pressure.

- Lie, threaten, or bluff in collaborative negotiations.

- Ignore the importance of relationship and likeability.

PRENEGOTIATION CHECKLIST

Are you ready for your negotiation? Want to make sure that everything goes as well as expected? Preparing for a negotiation is a major responsibility for the negotiation team. Team members will also need to pay attention to detail while planning the negotiation.

Follow this checklist to ensure a smooth and successful negotiation experience. You can tweak or update this checklist depending on your organization's unique needs. A thorough checklist will help you easily manage your negotiation.

Strategy

- ☐ Are you negotiating in zero-sum (positional)?

- ☐ Are you negotiating in a partnership (collaboration)?

- ☐ Are you negotiating in a SMARTnership (collaboration)?

- ☐ Share costs and benefits with your counterpart.

- ☐ Prepare a list of negotiable variables.

- ☐ Develop your agenda.

- ☐ Create and set the rules of the game.

- ☐ Determine your target, starting point, and threshold of pain.

Team

- ☐ Assign a lead, notetaker, and calculator.

- ☐ Determine if you have the authority to make decisions in the negotiation.

☐ Determine if the counterpart has the authority to make decisions.

☐ Determine how to utilize and support the team.

☐ Determine the roles in the counterpart's team.

Variables

☐ List all your variables.

☐ Determine your variables' costs and benefits.

☐ Determine your counterparts' variables, if possible.

☐ Decide if you will leave price and legal issue discussions to the end.

☐ Do not concede on a variable without getting something in return.

☐ Ask open-ended questions.

Process

☐ Minimize argumentation.

☐ Generate trust.

☐ Build a positive environment.

Planning Phase

☐ Attempt to create and identify new variables and direction for a deal during the negotiation.

☐ Balance information-sharing (don't give too much or too little).

☐ Take the initiative to open.

Bargaining

☐ Determine offers and counteroffers.

☐ Determine which concessions to make.

☐ Determine if you'll negotiate a goal as a whole or split it into smaller sizes (salami negotiation).

☐ Take a break, if necessary.

☐ Make sure you're following the agenda.

Communication

☐ Be confident.

☐ Be open.

☐ Create visual aids.

☐ Be aware of body language.

☐ Ask follow-up questions and summarize details.

Negotiation Style

☐ Determine what style to use (combative, collaborative, concessional, compromising, stalling).

☐ Be proactive in negotiating various points.

☐ Test limits of your counterpart (but avoid pushing too **hard**).

☐ Look at the complete picture and not the parts.

☐ Be open about the counterpart's input and comments.

☐ Ask open-ended questions.

Closing

☐ Minimize argumentation.

☐ Take the initiative to close the negotiation.

☐ Summarize points discussed, if necessary.

☐ Ask about anything the counterpart said that you didn't grasp or understand.

☐ Identify the split of NegoEconomics (asymmetric values) in the deal.

POSTNEGOTIATION EVALUATION CHECKLIST

How did it go? This is your opportunity to evaluate how the negotiation went. Here you can determine what went right, and what should be changed for next time. Write any specific notes in the Notes section.

Tweak or update this checklist depending on your organization's unique needs. A thorough checklist will help you easily manage your negotiation.

Roles Within the Group

☐ You had a leader, notetaker, and calculator.

☐ Kept discipline during the negotiation.

☐ Used SMARTnership (collaboration) to get to an end result.

☐ Team members were supportive to lead negotiator.

☐ Prepared list of negotiable variables.

☐ There was consensus on the deal within the team.

Summary of Negotiation

☐ Identified variables, including variables other than those prepared.

☐ Achieved negotiation goal.

☐ Reached threshold of pain.

☐ Found NegoEconomics in the deal.

☐ Capitalized on NegoEconomics of the deal.

☐ Was able to choose a style and change as needed.

Agenda

☐ Agenda was created.

☐ Followed the agenda.

The Negotiation Process

☐ Negotiation flowed without reaching a deadlock.

The Argumentation Phase

☐ Arguments were intelligible and credible.

☐ Focused on counterpart's values as well.

☐ There were no conflicts.

☐ Arguments produced results.

☐ Breaks were used effectively.

The Postmortem Phase

☐ All relevant input from the counterpart was taken into consideration.

☐ Every possible NegoEconomics variable was investigated.

☐ Counterpart's values and costs were clear to you.

- ☐ There was balance in the negotiation (not too much or too little information shared).

- ☐ Attempts were made to summarize and pin down points.

Conclusion

- ☐ Made the initiative to close the deal.

- ☐ Everyone agreed with demands made.

- ☐ Used all methods available to conclude the deal.

- ☐ Was aware of all parties' body language.

Communication

- ☐ You used one of the following styles: combative, collaborative, concessional, compromising, stalling.

- ☐ You used visual aids.

- ☐ There was credibility in the other party's points.

- ☐ Your points were credible.

- ☐ You asked questions.

- ☐ You followed up on questions.

- ☐ You summarized all values.

Negotiation Behavior

- ☐ Both parties were focused on establishing a positive environment.

- ☐ Both parties asked questions and moved the negotiation forward.

- ☐ You tested limits with the other party.

- ☐ You identified what could be improved for the next negotiation.

Notes

_____

_____

_____

_____

_____

_____

SMARTnership NEGOTIATION QUIZ

Let's test your new knowledge based on what you've learned in the book. You'll find the correct answers at the end. A correct answer will give you 5 points. If you score at least 90 points—congrats!—you've learned how to negotiate effectively. If you score below 90 points, I suggest revisiting the chapters where you got stuck.

1. **In negotiations, should the host always introduce the agenda?**

   a. Yes, the host should always present the agenda.

   b. The agenda is not important.

   c. The agenda should be negotiated by all parties.

2. **Can anyone else besides the negotiation leader comment during negotiations?**

   a. Only the leader should talk during negotiations.

   b. Yes, everyone can participate; however, it should be coordinated with the leader.

   c. Everyone should say what they want when they want.

3. **Can SMARTnership negotiations be conducted when there is a low level of trust?**

   a. No, it's difficult to generate the necessary openness if trust is lacking.

   b. Absolutely, trust is not required.

   c. Yes, if one party is unilateral and concession orientated.

4. **Which of the following best describes a zero-sum negotiation?**

    a. Everyone practices collaboration.

    b. Everyone stands up and yells.

    c. You either win at the expense of the counterpart, or no one wins.

5. **Describe NegoEconomics (negotiation economics).**

    a. The asymmetric value between your cost and the counterpart's value or vice versa

    b. Bribery

    c. The profit you make in the negotiation

6. **What is the real potential for generating financial value through NegoEconomics?**

    a. 14 percent

    b. 86 percent

    c. 42 percent

7. **How many dedicated types of negotiators exist?**

    a. 3: collaborative, positional, and conciliator

    b. 5: combative, collaborative, concessional, compromising, stalling

    c. 2: combative and aggressive

8. **How many phases are there in a successful negotiation?**

   a. 4

   b. 12

   c. 10

9. **How do you avoid unilateral concessions?**

   a. Start yelling.

   b. Ask questions and counterquestions.

   c. Give what the counterpart wants.

10. **What is a salami negotiation?**

    a. A negotiation that drags out

    b. A negotiation that is completed quickly

    c. A negotiation in which one or both parties divide the negotiation into portions

11. **How many negotiations is the average person involved in each year?**

    a. 800 to 1,000

    b. Around 5,000

    c. 8,000 to 10,000

12. **Which of the following is a variable that usually doesn't create NegoEconomics?**

    a. Price

b. Delivery time

c. Installation

13. **Tru$tCurrency is**

    a. Total cost of ownership

    b. The value of trust in a negotiation

    c. Total cost to others

14. **What will stress in a negotiation lead to?**

    a. Combativeness or concession (fight-or-flight mode)

    b. Collaboration

    c. Better planning

15. **If you negotiate virtually, what should you always do?**

    a. Negotiate by email.

    b. Negotiate using an online conference tool with a camera like Zoom, Teams, or similar.

    c. Send a letter by post office.

16. **What is the most common reason for not being able to capitalize on NegoEconomics?**

    a. Lack of openness

    b. Multicultural negotiations

    c. Not using the negotiation planner

17. **Why is arguing most often negative for developing value?**

    a. The counterpart will get sad.

    b. We are defending our viewpoint instead of being open for possibilities.

    c. We confuse ourselves.

18. **What should you do when meeting a combative negotiator?**

    a. Fight back.

    b. Ask questions.

    c. Use unilateral concessions.

19. **When is it OK to be a conceding negotiator?**

    a. When you want to make friends

    b. When you're confused about your strategy

    c. As a tactical move to gain goodwill

20. **Which one of these is a negotiation strategy?**

    a. SMARTnership

    b. A meeting

    c. A combative situation

Correct answers:

1c, 2b, 3a, 4c, 5a, 6c, 7b, 8c, 9b, 10c, 11c, 12a, 13b, 14a, 15b, 16a, 17b, 18b, 19c, 20a

Notes

Chapter 2

1. Jensen, K. "Forget Bitcoin; Trust Currency Is the New Currency That Will Make You Wealthy," *Forbes*, April 21, 2018. https://www.forbes.com/sites/keldjensen /2018/04/21/forget-bitcoin-trust-currency-is-the-new-currency-that-will-make -you-wealthy/?sh=3ef24e2d3324.

2. "Restoring trust: how to unlock the true potential of your organization," Kearney .com, May 29, 2013. https://www.kearney.com/leadership-change-organization /article/-/insights/restoring-trust-how-to-unlock-the-true-potential-of-your -organization.

3. "World Happiness, Trust and Social Connections," World Happiness Report, March 20, 2023. https://worldhappiness.report/ed/2023/world-happiness-trust -and-social-connections-in-times-of-crisis/#ranking-of-happiness-2020-2022.

4. Kahneman, D. *Thinking, Fast and Slow*. New York: Farrar, Straus, Giroux, 2011.

5. Grant, A. "In Negotiations, Givers Are Smarter Than Takers," *New York Times*, March 27, 2020.

Chapter 4

1. Jensen, K., & T. Cummins. "Online vs. Face-to-Face Negotiations," January 23, 2021. www.worldcc.com.

2. Morris, M., J. Nadler, T. Kurtzberg, & L. Thompson. "Schmooze or lose: Social friction and lubrication in E-mail negotiations," Northwestern University Scholars, Northwestern University, 2002. https://www.scholars.northwestern.edu/en/pub lications/schmooze-or-lose-social-friction-and-lubrication-in-e-mail-negoti.

3. Mehrabian, A. "Key Theories," British Library, 1967. https://www.bl.uk/people /albert-mehrabian.

4. Ibid.

5. Sinaceur, M., W. Maddux, D. Vasiljevic, R. Perez Nückel, & A. Galinsky. "Good things come to those who wait: late first offers facilitate creative agreements in negotiation," PubMed, June 2013. https://pubmed.ncbi.nlm.nih.gov/23696126/.

Chapter 10

1. Jensen, K. "The Biggest 1,000 Companies Could Be Losing $3.25 Trillion Annually—Here Is How to Avoid That," *Forbes*, April 30 2018. https://www.forbes.com/sites/keldjensen/2018/04/30/the-fortune-1000-could-be-loosing-325-trillion-annually-here-is-how-to-get-them/?sh=761ac31029ec.

2. Jensen, K. "Happy With 42% Less in Your Negotiations?," LinkedIn, April 26, 2022. https://www.linkedin.com/pulse/happy-42-less-your-negotiations-keld-jensen/?trk=portfolio_article-card_title.

Chapter 11

1. "These are the skills employers are looking for now . . . right up till 2025," WEF Future of Jobs Report 2020, Muchskills, January 19, 2022. https://www.muchskills.com/blog/skills-employers-looking-for-till-2025.

2. Fillmore, C. Speakers Gold, 2021, https://speakersgold.com.

3. Jensen, K. "The Biggest 1,000 Companies Could Be Losing $3.25 Trillion Annually—Here Is How to Avoid That," *Forbes*, April 30, 2018, https://www.forbes.com/sites/keldjensen/2018/04/30/the-fortune-1000-could-be-loosing-325-trillion-annually-here-is-how-to-get-them/?sh=20a629ec29ec.

Chapter 13

1. Carnegie, D. *How to Win Friends & Influence People.* New York: Simon & Schuster, 1936.

Index

About the Author

Keld Jensen is an internationally recognized and award-winning expert, TEDx speaker, author, and advisor on negotiation. He is the founder and head of Center for SMARTnership Negotiation, a consulting and training organization that works with private industry and governmental bodies to achieve greater levels of success through optimized solutions to complex problems. His clients include Vestas, Novo Nordisk, Johnson & Johnson, Carlsberg Group, Siemens, Rolls-Royce, LEGO, Bang & Olufsen, UCLA, UNICEF, ThermoFisher, World 50, and the governments of Canada, Denmark, and Great Britain.

Keld's background is primarily in management, including serving as CEO of PC Express AB, a publicly traded technology company. He is an associate professor and teaches at top-ranked universities around the world, including the Thunderbird School of Global Management at ASU, the BMI Executive Institute in Lithuania, BMI/Louvain University in Belgium, and Denmark's Aalborg University. He has lectured frequently at Copenhagen Business School and served as chairman of the school's Center for Negotiation.

Keld has made more than 200 international TV appearances, contributes regularly to *Forbes*, and has published hundreds of articles in other major business publications in Europe, Asia Pacific, and the United States. Keld is also a prolific author with 24 books, several of which have won awards. His works are available in more than 35 countries and 16 languages, with more than 2.8 million readers. In addition, Keld has long been an active mentor to entrepreneurs from small and medium-sized businesses, assisting in the creation of dozens of new companies and helping many more to grow and flourish through vital negotiations.

He was nominated as one of the world's 100 Top Thought Leaders in Trust for 2016; has been accepted on the prestigious Global Gurus Top 30 in 2021, 2022, and 2023; and is the creator of the world's most awarded negotiation strategy, winning the best negotiation strategy from the Organization of Public Procurement Officers in Denmark, awarded The World Commerce & Contracting Organization's Innovation and Strategic Award.

Keld is a dual citizen of the Kingdom of Denmark and the United States, where he resides. He has a wonderful wife with whom he has two children who improve his negotiation skills on a daily basis.

You can visit www.smartnershipclass.com for online training.